With an Everlasting Love

Developing an Intimate Relationship with God

William A. Barry, S.J.

Paulist Press
New York / Mahwah, N.J.

Acknowledgments

Excerpts from *A Marginal Jew: Rethinking the Historical Jesus* by John P. Meier, copyright © 1991 by John P. Meier, is used by permission of Doubleday, a division of Random House, Inc. Excerpts from *Mariette in Ecstasy* by Ron Hansen, copyright © 1991 by Ron Hansen, and from *The Longing for Home* by Frederick Buechner, copyright © 1996 by Frederick Buechner, are reprinted by permission of HarperCollins Publishers. Material from *The Spiritual Exercises of St. Ignatius,* translated by George E. Ganss, S.J., is reprinted by permission of the Institute of Jesuit Sources. Permission has been received to reprint excerpts from *The Collected Works of St. Teresa of Avila,* translated by Kieran Kavanaugh and Otilio Rodriguez, Volume One © 1976 and Volume Two © 1980, both by Washington Province of Discalced Carmelites, ICS Publications, 2131 Lincoln Road, N.E., Washington, D.C. 20002 USA. Excerpts from *God Is No Illusion: Meditations on the End of Life* by John Tully Carmody, copyright © 1997 by Trinity Press International, are reprinted by permission of Trinity Press International, Harrisburg, Pennsylvania. Excerpts from *The Poems of St. John of the Cross,* translated by Willis Barnstone, copyright © 1972 by New Directions Publishing Corp., are reprinted by permission of New Directions Publishing Corp. "Scaffolding" by Seamus Heaney is reprinted from his book *Poems 1965–1975,* copyright © 1980 by Seamus Heaney, by permission of Farrar, Straus & Giroux, Inc., New York, and Faber & Faber, London. The excerpt from "A Father's Story" by Andre Dubus is reprinted from *Broken Vessels,* copyright © 1991 by Andre Dubus, by permission of David R. Godine, Publisher, Inc. Scripture quotations are from the **New Revised Standard Version of the Bible,** copyright 1989 by the Division of Christian Education of the National Council of Churches of Christ in the USA. Used by permission. All rights reserved.

Imprimi Potest
Very Reverend Robert J. Levens, S.J., Provincial, Society of Jesus of New England

Library of Congress Cataloging-in-Publication Data

Barry, William A.
    With an everlasting love : developing an intimate relationship with God / William A. Barry.
      p. cm.
    Includes bibliographical references.
    ISBN 0-8091-3892-1 (alk. paper)
    1. Spiritual life—Catholic authors. I. Title.
BX2350.2.B3248   1999
248.4'82—dc21   99-37973
                                                       CIP

Published by Paulist Press
997 Macarthur Boulevard
Mahwah, New Jersey 07430

www.paulistpress.com

Printed and bound in the United States of America

Contents

iii

To Jack McCall, mentor
and
The Class of '48 of St. John's High School
on our 50th Anniversary

Preface

Teach me to seek You,
and reveal Yourself to me as I seek;
for unless You instruct me
I cannot seek You,
and unless You reveal Yourself
I cannot find You.
Let me seek You in desiring You;
let me desire You in seeking You.
Let me find You in loving You;
let me love You in finding You.

Writing this book has itself been a prayer. Each time that I opened the document containing the draft, I saw on my computer screen this prayer of St. Anselm of Canterbury, a remarkable prayer not only for its content, but also for its place in his work. He says this prayer just before he begins his ontological argument for the existence of God. For Anselm, obviously, writing such a philosophical work was a prayer. I have tried to take my cue from him. Each day before I began to write, I would say this prayer. Often, too, my day would begin with some question about the book that I would ask God during my morning prayer walk. Thus, the writing itself seemed to me to be a prayer. By the end of the book my relationship with the Lord had deepened. I hope that the book reflects God's desires and hopes for me and for the readers. It is a hope,

1

not a certainty, but I trust that the Spirit of God has led me during these months while the book was coming to birth.

My trust has been bolstered by the friends who have so generously read and commented on the various drafts. I am particularly grateful to Lawrence E. Corcoran, S.J., Robert G. Doherty, S.J., Marika Geoghegan, William C. Russell, S.J., and Madeline Tiberii, S.S.J., who very generously read the chapters as I completed drafts and made insightful and encouraging comments. Bob Doherty was especially helpful in his suggestions for improving both the style and the content. My spiritual director, Anne Harvery, S.N.D., not only has been unrelenting in prodding me toward a deeper relationship with the Lord, but also read the chapters as I finished the first drafts. Mary C. Guy and Philomena Sheerin, M.M.M., read the first draft of chapters 1 through 4 during a trip to Ireland and gave me solid and helpful feedback. Richard J. Clifford, S.J., provided very helpful leads to texts in the Old Testament and to works on the Old Testament and generously loaned me his own copies of the books on the Old Testament to which I refer. On a vacation trip James M. Collins, S.J., listened patiently as I expressed my enthusiasm for the work of N. T. Wright and read and discussed with me the three chapters on intimacy with Jesus. Daniel J. Harrington, S.J., assured me that my enthusiasm for N. T. Wright's work was not misplaced and read the chapters on intimacy with Jesus with his usual care and attention to detail. Rosalie J. Anderson proved once again that she is a proofreader without peer and a discriminating reader. None of these friends can be blamed for my failings, but they are responsible for saving me from not a few blunders and from some poor and unclear writing. I thank them from the bottom of my heart.

I also want to thank Don Brophy of Paulist Press, who suggested that I try my hand at a book on intimacy with

God and suggested as the central metaphor "seeing the face of God" from Psalm 42. He has been most encouraging.

I would encourage readers to make the prayer of St. Anselm their own as they make their way through the book. As I prayed my way through the writing, I learned more about God and God's desires for us. For example, only during the writing did I rediscover the image of the Trinity as dance, a dance to which we are invited. I hope that readers will also discover new aspects of God's desire for a relationship of intimacy. God has loved us with an everlasting love, gives us the desire for union and will fulfill that desire.

Chapter 1

Introduction

"I have loved you with an everlasting love; therefore I have continued my faithfulness to you" (Jer 31:30). Thus does God speak to his people, Israel, and to us who are the new Israel. God wants to be intimately related with each one of us individually and as a people. What about us? "As a deer longs for flowing streams, so my soul longs for you, O God. My soul thirsts for God, for the living God. When shall I come and behold the face of God?" (Ps 42:1–2). The fact that you are reading this book indicates that these words of the psalmist may express something of your own heart. There is no doubt that many people these days are experiencing a hunger for something more, a desire for "they know not what." I believe that this hunger is a hunger for God, a hunger that is the deepest desire of the human heart. We are made by God for God, and nothing but union with God will ultimately satisfy us. For some years now I have been exploring the issue of this hunger for God and have used the image of an intimate human relationship to do so. In this book I propose to explore this image in some depth. I hope that this exploration will be a help to you, the reader, in your own search for a more intimate relationship with God.

5

We will pursue the topic of intimacy with God both in terms of God's desire and initiative and in terms of the human desire and initiative. Scripture will be the primary reference, but I shall also refer to other literature and to my own and others' experience. We begin with the question: "What does God desire?" and then move on to: "What do I desire?" Throughout the book we will switch back and forth between the divine and human sides of the relationship.

Obviously, when we speak of a relationship of intimacy with God, we are using an analogy. The analogue is a human relationship. Let's reflect for some moments on the development of any intimate relationship. How do you get to know another person? First, you have to be interested in that person, to be attracted to her. You will not be tempted to spend time with another person if you are not in some way interested in her. Then, given the initial interest, you take some initiative to be with her, to get to know her. At first, the attempts may just be exploratory; you may begin talking about the weather or some other topic that will start the ball rolling. But if the relationship is to get off the ground, you will want to know something about her, and you hope that she will want to know something about you. Relationships develop through mutual self-revelation.

In the beginning these self-revelations tend to be rather superficial. "Where are you from?" "Where did you go to school?" "What do you do?" These are the kinds of questions that elicit information about the other. Eventually, of course, if both of you want to deepen the relationship, you will want to know more about each other's heart; not only "How many brothers and sisters do you have?" but also "How do you like them?"; not only "Where did you go to school?" but also "How did you like it there? What happened to you there?" As you get to know one another better, you will want to explore deeper values and beliefs.

Rather quickly, of course, you will want to know how you feel about each other. Hence, you will begin to communicate your reactions to each other. The relationship will continue to deepen as long as the two of you become more and more transparent, one with the other. Eventually, you may want to do something together—marry and start a family, or work together on a common project. Moreover, such a relationship will have its ups and downs; at times you will feel very close; at other times you will feel estranged. Continued development of the relationship will require that you learn how to trust each other with your negative as well as your positive feelings. You can do this only if you have established a firm foundation for the relationship, a foundation that can weather the eventual storms that arise in any relationship of intimacy.

A poem by Seamus Heaney, called "Scaffolding," is instructive about relationships.

> Masons, when they start upon a building,
> Are careful to test out the scaffolding;
> Make sure that planks won't slip at busy points,
> Secure all ladders, tighten bolted joints.
> And yet all this comes down when the job's done
> Showing off walls of sure and solid stone.
> So if, my dear, there sometimes seem to be
> Old bridges breaking between you and me
> Never fear. We may let the scaffolds fall
> Confident that we have built our wall.

Those who know the Spiritual Exercises of Ignatius of Loyola will be reminded of the "First Principle and Foundation," which serves as the introduction to the journey of developing a deeper relationship with God. Let us now see how well the analogy of a relationship of intimacy works when we speak of relating with the Creator of the universe.

I.

What Does God Want? What Do We Want?

Chapter 2

What Does God Want?

In Psalm 42 we read of the desire of the psalmist for God. "As a deer longs for flowing streams, so my soul longs for you, O God. My soul thirsts for God, for the living God. When shall I come and behold the face of God?" Before we explore this desire of the human heart, it might be good to ask ourselves what God desires in our regard.

Why did God create the universe and us human beings? Since we are asking about the divine intent here, only God can let us know. In human relationships I may infer from your actions and your demeanor what you intend, but I can easily be mistaken, especially if I do not know you well. Have you ever gotten angry when someone attributed motives to you that did not fit the bill? Just one example: The Enneagram, a nine-point kind of personality system, can be a very helpful way of understanding oneself and others. Many people have made workshops on the Enneagram. Some of them (too many, to my way of thinking) seem to think that they can then tell all their friends, acquaintances and even strangers what number in the Enneagram system they are. I find this tendency aggravating, especially when they want to tell me what number I am. As far as I can tell, the only way that anyone can be sure what number on the Enneagram I am (or anyone else, for that matter) is by my willingness to reveal to him or her my deeper motives, fears and anxieties. In other words, the only way that we can be certain of another's intentions is by his/her willingness to reveal them to us. We cannot know them for certain without a personal revelation. How much more true this is of the Creator! We can know God's intention in creation only through divine revelation. What do we learn of that intention from the scriptures, our primary source of knowledge of God's revelation?

The story of creation itself gives us an inkling that human beings are created for intimate conversation with God. The climax of the creation of the world comes with the creation of human beings, after which "God saw everything that he had made, and indeed, it was very good" (Gn 1:31).

> "Let us make humankind in our image, according to our likeness; and let them have dominion over the fish of the sea, and over the birds of the air, and over the cattle, and over all the wild animals of the earth, and over every creeping thing that creeps upon the earth." So God created humankind in his image, in the image of God he created them; male and female he created them. God blessed them, and God said to them, "Be fruitful and multiply, and fill the earth and subdue it; and have dominion over the fish of the sea and over the birds of the air and over every living thing that moves upon the earth." (Gn 1:26–28)

The Creator, it seems, creates human beings with some similarity to himself. The Hebrew text, however, may mean that God creates human beings similar to the angels who make up heaven's court and who are the divine messengers and representatives in the Hebrew scriptures. Even if this is

the meaning of the text, these angels are sometimes interchangeable with God in the stories of the Old Testament.
For example, in Genesis 18 we read: "The Lord appeared to
Abraham by the oaks of Mamre, as he sat at the entrance
of his tent in the heat of the day. He looked up and saw
three men standing near him. When he saw them, he ran
from the tent entrance to meet them, and bowed down to
the ground" (Gn 18:1–2). Here the three men or angels
and God seem interchangeable. These angels are on intimate terms with the Lord; they know God's desires and
intentions. If human beings are created in their image, the
presumption is that human beings are created for intimacy
with God. In addition, in this Genesis account human
beings are put in charge of the rest of creation. They take
the Creator's place on earth, acting as the sign of God's
rule of earth. God, then, seems to be revealing that we are
created for a close relationship with the Creator.

The second creation tradition, in chapters 2 and 3 of
Genesis, develops an even stronger image of an initial intimate relationship between Yahweh and the first human
beings. After the woman and the man have eaten of the
forbidden tree, we read: "They heard the sound of the Lord
God walking in the garden at the time of the evening
breeze" (Gn 3:8). Yahweh is depicted as dwelling in the
garden with the man and the woman and taking an
evening stroll. The assumption of the story is that God
expects to see the man and the woman and talk with them
since we read that on this occasion

> ...the man and his wife hid themselves from the pres-
> ence of the Lord God among the trees of the garden.
> But the Lord God called to the man, and said to him,
> "Where are you?" He said, "I heard the sound of you
> in the garden, and I was afraid, because I was naked;
> and I hid myself." (Gn 3:8–10)

Apparently before their disobedience they were not afraid to be in God's presence, even naked. Even now, after their sin, God addresses them directly. In fact, the question, "Where are you?" can be interpreted as a parent's query to a child, such as, "What are you up to now?" The story assumes that the disobedience of the man and the woman has disrupted a relationship of intimacy and ease between them and God. They are now afraid and hide themselves. The expulsion from the garden indicates the estrangement from a prior intimacy that their disobedience has brought about. (For some of the interpretation of the two Genesis traditions I have used E. A. Speiser's introduction and commentary in *The Anchor Bible. Genesis.*)

From the beginning of creation, it seems, we were made for divine intimacy. After the sin of disobedience does God still desire such intimacy? There are abundant indications in the Bible that the answer has to be yes. The Lord personally confronts Cain after he has murdered his brother Abel, an indication of continuing divine concern (Gn 4:8–16). When Yahweh is depicted as regretful that he had made human beings because of their wickedness, we are told that "Noah found favor in the sight of the Lord" (Gn 6:8). The Lord spoke directly with Noah, telling him to build the ark and to save his own family and two of each living creature. The Abraham cycle in the book of Genesis (chapters 12–18) strongly indicates God's continuing desire for an intimate relationship with human beings. Beginning with the call to Abraham in chapter 12 we read of a growing bond of intimacy between God and Abraham and Sarah, Abraham's wife.

These one-on-one conversations show how a mutual trust grew among them. For example, at one point God promises Abraham that he will have a son by Sarah. Abraham is ninety-nine and Sarah eighty-nine; Abraham

already has a son, Ishmael, by Sarah's maid, Hagar. What
is Abraham's reaction to God's promise?

> Then Abraham fell on his face and laughed, and said
> to himself, "Can a child be born to a man who is a hun-
> dred years old? Can Sarah, who is ninety years old,
> bear a child?" And Abraham said to God, "O that
> Ishmael might live in your sight!" God said, "No, but
> your wife Sarah shall bear you a son, and you shall
> name him Isaac. I will establish my covenant with him
> as an everlasting covenant for his offspring after him.
> As for Ishmael, I have heard you; I will bless him and
> make him fruitful and exceedingly numerous; he shall
> be the father of twelve princes, and I will make him a
> great nation. But my covenant I will establish with
> Isaac, whom Sarah shall bear to you at this season
> next year." And when he had finished talking with
> him, God went up from Abraham. (Gn 17:17–22)

Abraham is able to laugh out loud at God's preposterous
promise, asking the Lord, in effect, to get serious. Ishmael
is the only son he will have as an heir. God does not get
angry, but seems to get into the spirit of the conversation.
One can almost sense a smile in the words: "As for
Ishmael, I have heard you; I will bless him and make him
fruitful and exceedingly numerous; he shall be the father
of twelve princes, and I will make him a great nation." It is
as though God is saying: "OK, OK, I got it; I'll take care of
Ishmael. But your heir will be a son by Sarah."
In the next chapter the divine promise is repeated.

> They (the three men who represent God) said to him,
> "Where is your wife Sarah?" And he said, "There, in
> the tent." Then one said, "I will surely return to you in

due season, and your wife Sarah shall have a son."
And Sarah was listening at the tent entrance behind
him. Now Abraham and Sarah were old, advanced in
age; it had ceased to be with Sarah after the manner
of women. So Sarah laughed to herself, saying, "After
I have grown old, and my husband is old, shall I have
pleasure?" The Lord said to Abraham, "Why did
Sarah laugh, and say, 'Shall I indeed bear a child,
now that I am old?' Is anything too wonderful for the
Lord? At the set time I will return to you, in due season, and Sarah shall have a son." But Sarah denied,
saying, "I did not laugh"; for she was afraid. He said,
"Oh yes, you did laugh." (Gn 18:9–15)

One can easily imagine a humorous smile accompanying
the remark "Oh yes, you did laugh."
Now a remarkable story of divine self-revelation
unfolds.

Then the men (the three) set out from there, and they
looked toward Sodom; and Abraham went with them
to set them on their way. The Lord said, "Shall I hide
from Abraham what I am about to do, seeing that
Abraham shall become a great and mighty nation,
and all the nations of the earth shall be blessed in
him? No, for I have chosen him, that he may charge
his children and his household after him to keep the
way of the Lord by doing righteousness and justice; so
that the Lord may bring about for Abraham what he
has promised him."
Then the Lord said, "How great is the outcry
against Sodom and Gomorrah and how very grave
their sin! I must go down and see whether they have
done altogether according to the outcry that has
come to me; and if not, I will know." So the men

turned from there, and went toward Sodom, while Abraham remained standing before the Lord. Then Abraham came near and said, "Will you indeed sweep away the righteous with the wicked? Suppose there are fifty righteous within the city; will you then sweep away the place and not forgive it for the fifty righteous who are in it? Far be it from you to do such a thing, to slay the righteous with the wicked, so that the righteous fare as the wicked! Far be that from you! Shall not the Judge of all the earth do what is just?" (Gn 18:17–25)

God decides to reveal to Abraham his decision to destroy Sodom, opening the divine heart in such a way that Abraham can interfere. Abraham proceeds to tell God how to act, indeed, to chide the Lord for thinking of acting in an ungodlike way. It is a remarkable instance of the divine desire for an intimate relationship with a human being. It leads to the haggling between the two of them that ends when the Lord promises not to destroy the cities if ten righteous people can be found in them.

Moses was also one to whom God spoke intimately. In Exodus 33:11 we read: "Thus the Lord used to speak to Moses face to face, as one speaks to a friend." He, too, grew in trust in this relationship so that he could bargain with God to protect the Israelites (Ex 32:31).

In addition to these and like stories of individuals called to an intimate divine relationship, we also find instances of God's tender love and desire for the whole people of Israel, a love and desire that seem to want a tender closeness. Indeed, the choice of individuals like Abraham and Moses as intimates of God seems to be dictated by God's desire to draw a whole people, and finally the whole world, into an intimate relationship. For those of us immersed in a culture of individualism, it is a good corrective to realize that God desires intimacy with a whole people, as a people as well as individuals. Moses tells the people why the Lord chose them as his own.

> It was not because you were more numerous than any other people that the Lord set his heart on you and chose you—for you were the fewest of all peoples. It was because the Lord loved you and kept the oath that he swore to your ancestors, that the Lord has brought you out with a mighty hand, and redeemed you from the house of slavery, from the hand of the Pharaoh king of Egypt. Know therefore that the Lord your God is God, the faithful God who maintains covenant loyalty with those who love him and keep his commandments, to a thousand generations, and who repays in their own person those who reject him. (Dt 7:7–10)

This covenental relationship is expressed in love and loyalty on both sides. As we shall see, it was a turbulent relationship because of Israel's infidelity. But through all its stormy history God continually expresses a personal fidelity and a repeated desire for Israel's mutual fidelity and love.

With the coming of Emmanuel, God-With-Us, in Jesus we discover that God wants to have such a bonding with all human beings. Whatever the divine predilection for Israel prior to the coming of Christ meant, it seems clear from the New Testament that God now makes his covenant with all human beings no matter their race, culture or family background. Jesus believed that the people of Israel were to be a light to the Gentiles, a light that they should not put under a bushel (cf. Mt 5:14–16). In John's gospel Jesus prays to his Father at the last supper:

> After Jesus had spoken these words, he looked up to heaven and said, "Father, the hour has come; glorify your Son so that the Son may glorify you, since you have given him authority over all people, to give eternal life to all whom you have given him. And this is eternal life, that they may know you, the only true God, and Jesus Christ whom you have sent." (Jn 17:1–3)

Here the word *know* means to know and love, to know intimately. Indeed, in the Bible the word *know* is also used of sexual intercourse. In the First Letter to Timothy the author writes: "This is right and is acceptable in the sight of God our Savior, who desires everyone to be saved and to come to the knowledge of the truth. For there is one God; there is also one mediator between God and humankind, Christ Jesus, himself human, who gave himself a ransom for all" (1 Tm 2:3–6). Of course, there were intimations of the universal love of God even in the Hebrew Bible. For example, the book of Jonah is predicated on the notion that God loves the people of Nineveh, who are not Jewish. In addition, the author of the Wisdom of Solomon (a book written in Greek in Alexandria near the beginning of the Christian era and considered part of the Bible by Roman Catholics and other Christians), says to God:

> Because the whole world before you is like a speck that tips the scales, and like a drop of morning dew that falls on the ground. But you are merciful to all, for you can do all things, and you overlook people's sins, so that they may repent. For you love all things that exist, and detest none of the things that you have made, for you would not have made anything if you had hated it. How would anything have endured if you had not willed it? Or how would anything not

called forth by you have been preserved? You spare
all things, for they are yours, O Lord, you who love
the living. (Wis 11:22–26)

God wants all human beings to be part of the one family of
God.

We Christians believe that Jesus is the final revelation of
what his Father wants in this world. In the gospels Jesus
continually speaks of the coming of God's kingdom, a coming that is already present in his own life and ministry. The
kingdom of God signifies the triumph of God's dream for
this world. But what does the kingdom of God mean? What
does God want and continue to pursue actively through all
of history? It would seem that the Creator brings each
human being into existence for union with the Trinity,
which includes unity with all other human beings and with
all of creation. (I have developed this idea at some length
in *Who Do You Say I Am?*, chapter 3.)

Do we have inklings in our own experience that point to
this divine desire for us and our world? Have you ever
experienced a time of great inner and outer harmony and
felt a surge of poignant joy? For example, at a moment of
reconciliation between family members who had been at
odds, or at a religious service of reconciliation where
people of varied races and cultures celebrated together. I
have been moved to tears of such poignant joy at the grad-
uation ceremony at Nativity Prep School in the inner city
of Boston, where boys of various racial and ethnic back-
grounds speak of the love for one another that has developed during their years of studying and playing together.

The writer Frederick Buechner describes such an experience in *The Longing for Home.* He and his wife and daughter were visiting Sea World in Orlando on a beautiful day;
he admits it is an unlikely place for an experience of God.

The bleachers were packed as six killer whales were released into the tank.

> What with the dazzle of the sky and sun, the beautiful young people on the platform, the soft southern air, and the crowds all around us watching the performance with a delight matched only by what seemed the delight of the performing whales, it was as if the whole creation—men and women and beasts and sun and water and earth and sky and, for all I know, God himself—was caught up in one great, jubilant dance of unimaginable beauty. And then, right in the midst of it, I was astonished to find that my eyes were filled with tears.

His wife and daughter had a similar experience. Buechner goes on to write:

> I believe there is no mystery about why we shed tears. We shed tears because we had caught a glimpse of the Peaceable Kingdom, and it had almost broken our hearts. For a few moments we had seen Eden and been part of the great dance that goes on at the heart of creation. We shed tears because we were given a glimpse of the way life was created to be and is not. We had seen why it was the "morning stars sang together, and all the sons of God shouted for joy" when the world was first made, as the book of Job describes it, and of what it was that made Saint Paul write, even when he was in prison and on his way to execution, "Rejoice in the Lord always; again I will say, Rejoice." We had had a glimpse of part at least of what Jesus meant when he said, "Blessed are you that weep now, for you shall laugh."

I interpret such experiences as the experience of God's creative touch drawing us toward the dream that is God's desire for our world and for each one of us. God wants to draw us into union with the community life that is the Trinity, a community life that is inclusive of all human beings. When, like Buechner and his family, we catch a glimpse of the Peaceable Kingdom, we are in touch with God's dream for our universe and for us.

We Christians also profess that Jesus is the incarnation of God in this world, that Jesus is God-for-us and God-with-us. In the gospels Jesus is depicted as calling men and women into a relationship of friendship. During the last discourse in John's gospel Jesus speaks to his disciples:

> "As the Father has loved me, so I have loved you; abide in my love. If you keep my commandments, you will abide in my love, just as I have kept my Father's commandments and abide in his love. I have said these things to you so that my joy may be in you, and that your joy may be complete.
>
> "This is my commandment, that you love one another as I have loved you. No one has greater love than this, to lay down one's life for one's friends. You are my friends if you do what I command you. I do not call you servants any longer, because the servant does not know what the master is doing; but I have called you friends, because I have made known to you everything that I have heard from my Father." (Jn 15:9–15)

If Jesus calls them friends, then God calls them friends. And note that friendship means complete transparency. In the Abraham cycle the reciprocity of transparency between God and Abraham becomes clear in the story of their haggling over the fate of Sodom and Gomorrah. At the last supper Jesus calls his disciples friends because he has made known to them everything he has heard from the Father. There is no reason to restrict Jesus' desire for friendship to these few disciples. Down the centuries Christians have read these words and believed and felt that they were directed to them. God wants our friendship.

In the final exercise of the *Spiritual Exercises* Ignatius of Loyola has the retreatant reflect in this way:

> I will call back into my memory the gifts I have received—my creation, redemption, and other gifts particular to myself. I will ponder with deep affection how much God our Lord has done for me, and how much he has given me of what he possesses, and consequently how he, the same Lord, desires to give me even his very self, in accordance with his divine design.

Ignatius came to believe, as have many saints, that the Creator desires the deepest intimacy possible with us human creatures. The only limit on that desire is our capacity to receive the divine fullness. Another translation of the last line strikes me as expressing a sense of poignancy: "...it is the Lord's wish, as far as he is able, to give me himself." One can almost feel God's wish that we could receive all of himself.

Finally, let us return to the image of the Trinity inviting us into their intimate life. Many readers will have seen reproductions of the famous icon of the Trinity painted by Andrei Rublev, the Russian iconographer, about 1411. He used the image of the three men who visited Abraham to depict the three Persons of God sitting at table pointing to the chalice, the symbol of their overflowing love. There is a place at this table for the viewer. Anyone who views this icon feels invited to sit down with the three Persons to share the divine community and communion. Perhaps there is no more fitting image to end this chapter in which we have been asking what God desires in our regard. The invitation is to sit down at that heavenly banquet, commune intimately with the three Persons whose essence is to be in intimate relationship with one another in the one God.

Chapter 3

The Deepest Desire
of the Human Heart

"Then we can ask reverently of our lover whatever we will. For by nature our will wants God, and the good will of God wants us. We shall never cease wanting and longing until we possess him in fullness and joy. Then we shall have no further wants." So writes Julian of Norwich in her *Revelations of Divine Love*. She is only echoing others like Augustine of Hippo who, in his *Confessions*, wrote: "The thought of you stirs him [a human being] so deeply that he cannot be content unless he praises you, because you made us for yourself and our hearts find no peace until they rest in you" (I, 1, p. 21). Do you experience this longing for God? Perhaps the fact that you have this book in your hands is an indication that you do experience such a longing. In this chapter we will look at the desire for God as the deepest desire of the human heart.

The scriptures seem to presume the truth of the statements of Julian and Augustine. For example, the psalmist prays:

As a deer longs for flowing streams, so my soul longs for you, O God. My soul thirsts for God, for the living God. When shall I come and behold the face of God?

The rest of the psalm expresses his sorrow at being deprived of seeing the face of God, as in these lines.

My tears have been my food day and night, while people say to me continually, "Where is your God?" These things I remember, as I pour out my soul: how I went with the throng, and led them in procession to the house of God, with glad shouts and songs of thanksgiving, a multitude keeping festival. Why are you cast down, O my soul, and why are you disquieted within me? Hope in God; for I shall again praise him, my help and my God. My soul is cast down within me; therefore I remember you from the land of Jordan and of Hermon, from Mount Mizar. (Ps 42)

The psalmist's agony that God seems distant indicates the depth of his desire for God's presence.

Another psalm expresses the great desire for the presence of the Lord, seemingly in a time of great trouble.

One thing I asked of the Lord, that will I seek after: to live in the house of the Lord all the days of my life, to behold the beauty of the Lord, and to inquire in his temple....

Hear, O Lord, when I cry aloud, be gracious to me and answer me! "Come," my heart says, "seek his face!" Your face, Lord, do I seek. Do not hide your face from me. Do not turn your servant away in anger, you who have been my help. Do not cast me off, do not forsake me, O God of my salvation! If my father and mother

> forsake me, the Lord will take me up. Teach me your
> way, O Lord, and lead me on a level path because of
> my enemies. Do not give me up to the will of my
> adversaries, for false witnesses have risen against me,
> and they are breathing out violence. I believe that I
> shall see the goodness of the Lord in the land of the
> living. Wait for the Lord; be strong, and let your heart
> take courage; wait for the Lord! (Ps 27:5–14)

The poet of this psalm is enamored of God. He speaks of
the beauty of the Lord, and expresses strongly his desire to
see God's face. According to Samuel Terrien, the Hebrew
word translated as "beauty" is related to words that
"apply to physical charm, erotic and aesthetic enjoyment,
the various emotions of friendship, the thrill of learning,
and the holy pleasure of liturgical singing." The psalmist's
yearning for God's presence is strong indeed. The thought
of being deprived of it is a source of deep pain. The same
passionate desire for God is expressed in Psalm 63: "O
God, you are my God, I seek you, my soul thirsts for you;
my flesh faints for you, as in a dry and weary land where
there is no water" (Ps 63:1).

Apparently the poet who wrote Psalm 84 was in exile
from the temple; he expresses his sense of homelessness,
far from the Lord. His desire for the "courts of the Lord" is
a desire for nearness to God.

> How lovely is your dwelling place, O Lord of hosts!
> My soul longs, indeed it faints for the courts of the
> Lord; my heart and my flesh sing for joy to the living
> God. Even the sparrow finds a home, and the swallow
> a nest for herself, where she may lay her young, at
> your altars, O Lord of hosts, my King and my God.
> Happy are those who live in your house, ever singing
> your praise.

Happy are those whose strength is in you, in whose heart are the highways to Zion. As they go through the valley of Baca they make it a place of springs; the early rain also covers it with pools. They go from strength to strength; the God of gods will be seen in Zion. O Lord God of hosts, hear my prayer; give ear, O God of Jacob!

Behold our shield, O God; look on the face of your anointed. For a day in your courts is better than a thousand elsewhere. I would rather be a doorkeeper in the house of my God than live in the tents of wickedness. For the Lord God is a sun and shield; he bestows favor and honor. No good thing does the Lord withhold from those who walk uprightly. O Lord of hosts, happy is everyone who trusts in you. (Ps 84)

This psalm has been set to music by the St. Louis Jesuits and is often sung in modern liturgies. When we sing the song, "One thing I ask, this alone I seek, to dwell in the house of the Lord all my days," does it express a real desire of our hearts? Do these texts speak to my own experience? Do I, at times, experience something like this strong desire for "I know not what," for God?

In his final illness my friend, the theologian and writer John Carmody, wrote a number of psalms that were edited and published by his wife after his death. In one of them he expressed his love for God openly while admitting that his love was imperfect.

You give us two commands
and let them merge into one.
We are to love you with all our heart
and to love our neighbors as ourselves.
More simply, we are to love always and everywhere:
our friends and our enemies,
the skies above and the earth under our feet.

For you are love,
and those who abide in love abide in you.
It could not be plainer, more sharply focused:
the greatest of your gifts is love;
love is our only crucial obligation.
I love you, God, and have for all my adult life.
I love you badly, distractedly, impurely,
but from the first I knew what your name meant,
first received the slightest inkling,
I knew you were all I needed or wanted
and my life gained purpose and order.
What shall I return to you
for all the favors that loving you has brought me?
I shall dwell in the thought of you,
the hope for you,
the trust in your care for me,
and the love that you pour forth in my heart
all the days of my life
and all your heaven to come.

In the scriptural texts we read the desire for God seems
not only to produce sadness that the desire is not fulfilled
but also to produce joy. "My soul longs, indeed it faints for
the courts of the Lord; my heart and my flesh sing for joy
to the living God." I am reminded of C. S. Lewis's autobio-
graphical memoir *Surprised by Joy*. The "joy" he is surprised
by is the desire for God, but for a long time he did not
know the object of the desire. He recounts one such experience of "joy":

As I stood before a flowering currant bush on a sum-
mer day there suddenly arose in me without warning,
and as if from a depth not of years but of centuries, the
memory of that earlier morning at the Old House
when my brother had brought his toy garden into the

nursery. It is difficult to find words strong enough for the sensation which came over me; Milton's "enormous bliss" of Eden...comes somewhere near it. It was a sensation, of course, of desire; but desire for what? not, certainly, for a biscuit tin filled with moss, nor even (though that came into it) for my own past....and before I knew what I desired, the desire itself was gone, the whole glimpse withdrawn, the world turned commonplace again, or only stirred by a longing for the longing that had just ceased. It had taken only a moment of time; and in a certain sense everything else that had ever happened to me was insignificant in comparison.

For years Lewis sought to satisfy this desire through other objects. Finally he realized that this desire he called "joy" was the desire for God. In another place he describes this "joy" as an intense longing that can be distinguished from other longings by two things. First, though the want is strong and even painful, still the desire itself is a delight. Here he echoes the psalmist. Second, we can be mistaken about the object of the desire, as Lewis himself was for a good part of his early life. The hunger for God, though unfulfilled completely in this life, is experienced as a delight, precisely as "joy."

In *Let This Mind Be in You* where he comments on Lewis's "joy," the desire for "I know not what," Sebastian Moore writes: "Now all desire is desire for intimacy, for a fulfilling situation of being with another or being part of some great project. Desire is for fuller life." He goes on to argue that this desire for "I know not what" is the result of the creative touch of God, the counterpart in human beings of God's desire, which brings them into existence and preserves them in existence. What God wants in creating the universe, in other words, creates in us a desire for what

God wants, namely, an intimate relationship of friendship and love. Have you felt the welling up of such a desire for "you knew not what" with the concomitant feeling of great well-being and even joy? If you have, then you have experienced the creative touch of God drawing you into an intimate relationship.

Augustine was echoing Christian faith when he affirmed that our hearts are made for God and are restless until they rest in God. This article of faith means that everyone must, at some time, and perhaps often, experience the desire for "I know not what." But people may not interpret the experience as the touch of God, as C. S. Lewis did not for many years. The experience can be interpreted in different ways. The mystery novelist P. D. James must know of this experience. In at least two of her novels she describes such experiences in characters who do not have religious faith. The descriptions are instructive. In *Original Sin,* one of her detective stories featuring Chief Inspector Dalgliesh, James writes of his subordinate, Kate Mishkin:

> Standing now between the glitter of the water and the high, delicate blue of the sky, she felt an extraordinary impulse which had visited her before and which she thought must be as close as she could ever get to a religious experience. She was possessed by a need, almost physical in its intensity, to pray, to praise, to say thank you, without knowing to whom, to shout with a joy that was deeper than the joy she felt in her own physical well-being and achievements or even in the beauty of the physical world.

The novelist is describing the experience of the desire for "I know not what," but Kate is not ready to interpret the experience as the touch of God drawing her to an intimate relationship.

In *Innocent Blood,* a quite different novel, James writes of her central character:

> Philippa sat absolutely still in the silence, and there began to flow through her a sense of tingling delight, entrancing in its strangeness. Even the inanimate objects in the room, the air itself, were suffused with this iridescent joy. She fixed her eyes on the geranium on the windowsill. Why had she never before realised how beautiful it was? She had seen geraniums as the gaudy expedient of municipal gardeners to be planted in park beds, massed on political platforms, a useful pot plant for the house, since it throve with so little attention. But this plant was a miracle of beauty. Each flowerlet was curled like a miniature rosebud on the end of its furred, tender stem. Imperceptibly but inevitably as her own breathing they were opening to the light. The petals were a clear, transparent pink, faintly striped with yellow, and the fan-like leaves, how intricately veined they were, how varied in their greenness, each with its darker penumbra. Some words of William Blake fell into her mind, familiar but new. "Everything that lives is holy. Life delights in life." Even her body's flux, which she could feel as a gentle, almost controlled, flow, wasn't the inconvenient and disagreeable monthly discharge of the body's waste. There was no waste. Everything living was part of one great wholeness. To breathe was to take delight. She wished that she knew how to pray, that there was someone to whom she could say: "Thank you for this moment of happiness. Help me to make her [her mother, a murderess] happy." And she thought of other words, familiar but untraceable to their source: "In whom we live and move and have our being."

While writing this chapter, I read *The Cunning Man,* a novel by Robertson Davies, who also must know of this experience of the desire for "I know not what." Chips, one of two English ladies who have come over to Canada together, writes sharp, witty letters to a friend in England. The protagonist of the novel has come into possession of the letters after her death and is using them as part of his story of what happened in the local Anglican church some years before. In one of them Chips describes her experience on an Easter Sunday.

> Then Saturday, a dead day in the church. Then Easter Day itself and a Mass at seven...and a High Mass at half past ten and such music and such ritual goings-on as you've never seen in your entire puff, and a magnificent spirit of life and love in a packed church.
>
> You felt it even before the procession. But when the choir burst into *The strife is o'er, the battle done; / Now is the Victor's triumph won; / O let the song of praise be sung; / Alleluya!* I swear to you I felt that for the first time in my life I knew what religion really meant! It was a kind of amazing lightness in the buzzem—O hell, I can't write about it in this campy slangy way I've got into—this way that tries to turn everything into a joke! It was no joke. But it wasn't religious-serious either. It was as though I'd been renewed and wouldn't need to play the fool all the time to hide real feeling. Lots of people were blubbing. And I felt as if for the first time I could just be me, and wouldn't have to play the giddy goat so that nobody could really get near me. I don't think I'm making much sense, but I hope I'm getting it across to you that it was a revelation. Am I now a believer, a religious person? I can't tell, but I know I've never felt like that before and want to feel that way forever.

Note that Chips writes that she wants to feel this way forever. The deepest desire of the human heart is for God.

Thus, it is not only mystics who yearn for God. The poet
George Herbert knew of the restlessness of the human
heart and in his poem "The Pulley" ascribes it to the goodness of the Creator.

When God at first made man,
Having a glass of blessings standing by,
Let us (said he) pour on him all we can:
Let the world's riches, which dispersed lie,
    Contract into a span.
    So strength first made a way;
Then beauty flow'd, then wisdom, honour, pleasure:
When almost all was out, God made a stay,
Perceiving that, alone of all his treasure,
    Rest in the bottom lay.
    For if I should (said he)
Bestow this jewel also on my creature,
He would adore my gifts instead of me,
And rest in Nature, not the God of Nature:
    So both should losers be.
    Yet let him keep the rest,
But keep them with restlessness;
Let him be rich and weary, that at least,
If goodness lead him not, yet weariness
    May toss him to my breast.

In Herbert's conceit God leaves our hearts restless for our
good. The line "So both should losers be" seems ambiguous
to me. It could mean that nature and human beings would
be losers if human beings rested in nature; but it could also
mean that the losers would be human beings and God. On
the latter reading God would be sad if we did not yearn for
union with him. That this may not be far from the mark

was brought home to me in my most recent retreat. I felt God saying to me, "It gives joy to my heart that you love me. It delights me." I found it hard to believe, but finally did. Implicit in the statement may be that God is saddened when we do not respond to him with love.

Perhaps all of us, if we were to pay attention to the movements of our hearts, would realize that Psalm 63 is our song: "O God, you are my God, I seek you, my soul thirsts for you; my flesh faints for you, as in a dry and weary land where there is not water," and that the words of one of the songs in the Song of Solomon describe our own deepest longing for God: "Upon my bed at night I sought him whom my soul loves; I sought him, but found him not; I called him, but he gave not answer....I will seek him whom my soul loves" (Sg 3:1-2).

A final note. The desire God planted in my heart will not be satisfied if I am the only one who attains the desire. We are inescapably relational, tied to family, close friends, their friends. Our desire for God includes the desire for the Peaceable Kingdom mentioned by Frederick Buechner. Another experience described by Buechner brings this home. He had just signed a contract for his first novel and was leaving the publisher's office when he ran into an acquaintance from college who was working as a messenger boy. In his memoir *The Sacred Journey* he recalled that moment:

> I was, as I thought, on the brink of fame and fortune. But instead of feeling any pride or sense of superior accomplishment by the comparison, I remember a great and unheralded rush of something like sadness, almost like shame. I had been very lucky, and he had not been very lucky, and the pleasure that I might have taken in what had happened to me was all but lost in the realization that nothing comparable, as far as I could see, had happened to him....All I can say

now is that something small but unforgettable happened inside me as the result of that chance meeting—some small flickering out of the truth that, in the
long run, there can be no real joy for anybody until
there is joy finally for us all—and I can take no credit
for it. It was nothing I piously thought my way to. It
was no conscious attempt to work out my own salvation. What I felt was something better and truer than
I was, or than I am, and it happened, as perhaps all
such things do, as a gift.

We shall let Julian of Norwich have the final word on this
topic. Near the end of her *Revelations of Divine Love* she
writes: "For the thirst of God is to include Everyman within
himself, and it is through this thirst that he has drawn his
holy ones into their present blessedness. He is ever drawing and drinking, as it were, as he gets these living members, yet he still thirsts and longs."

II.

Obstacles in the Way of Our Desire

Chapter 4

The Fear of God's Face

If it is true that God wants intimacy with us and that the deepest desire of our hearts is for intimacy with God, how can we explain our reluctance to engage in an intimate relationship with God? One woman wrote to me after a workshop on prayer: "I have always puzzled over why prayer, which is the one thing in the world I want most to do, is also the last thing I want to do." She then put down the reasons she had discovered, four pages of them. In addition to our own reluctance, how do we explain the many sayings in scripture about the necessary fear of God any human being should have?

The words of the Israelites to Moses might express the feelings of many people: "You speak to us, and we will listen; but do not let God speak to us, or we will die" (Ex 20:19). Later Israelites who read or heard the stories of David's kingship might have similar reactions to God's closeness. As David was taking the ark of God to his city, it apparently became unbalanced and Uzzah reached out to keep it from falling:

> When they came to the threshing floor of Nacon, Uzzah reached out his hand to the ark of God and

took hold of it, for the oxen shook it. The anger of the
Lord was kindled against Uzzah; and God struck him
there because he reached out his hand to the ark; and
he died there beside the ark of God. (2 Sm 6:6-7)

Who would want to get close to a God who would act in
such a violent and arbitrary way?

There is a persistent theme in the Hebrew Bible that no
one who sees the face of God can live. Gideon expresses
this fear when he cries out after perceiving that he has
been speaking with an angel of the Lord: "Help me, Lord
God! For I have seen the angel of the Lord face to face"
(Jgs 6:22). Moses, who became the great friend of God,
reacts with fear after having been attracted by the burning bush that was not consumed. "Moses hid his face, for
he was afraid to look at God" (Ex 3:6). Moreover, in a later
remarkable scene of intimacy between Moses and God,
God says to Moses:

> "I will make all my goodness pass before you, and will
> proclaim before you the name, 'The Lord'; and I will be
> gracious to whom I will be gracious, and will show
> mercy on whom I will show mercy. But," he said, "you
> cannot see my face; for no one shall see me and live."
> And the Lord continued, "See, there is a place by me
> where you shall stand on the rock; and while my glory
> passes by I will put you in a cleft of the rock, and I will
> cover you with my hand until I have passed by; then I
> will take away my hand, and you shall see my back; but
> my face shall not be seen." (Ex 33:19-23)

God seems to be saying that intimacy with him will
destroy Moses. Yet earlier in this very chapter, as we have
already noted, it is said: "Thus the Lord used to speak to

Moses face to face, as one speaks to a friend" (Ex 33:11). And in another place God chides the Israelites for their anger at Moses by saying: "Hear my words: When there are prophets among you, I the Lord make myself known to them in visions; I speak to them in dreams. Not so with my servant Moses; he is entrusted with all my house. With him I speak face to face—clearly, not in riddles; and he beholds the form of the Lord" (Nm 12:6–8). What are we to make of the seeming contradiction? First, we need to remember that the scriptures are God's word told through human words. Thus the mindset, the imagination, the biases and prejudices, the maturity of religious sensibility and other human factors of the storytellers and writers affect how God's revelation is received, understood and repeated down the ages. The story of Uzzah's death, for example, was probably told to exemplify the awesome power of Yahweh, a much stronger God than the gods of Israel's neighbors, and then was used by the compiler of the Second Book of Samuel as part of the dramatic tale of the bringing of the ark to David's capital of Jerusalem, an event that solidified David's kingship over Israel. Thus we need not take as literal truth that God became enraged at Uzzah for doing what came naturally when he saw that the ark was in danger of tipping. Nonetheless, the story does illustrate the dread that the notion of God's closeness brought out in the Israelites. Second, we need to look at ourselves. Do we ourselves have some deep-seated dread of God's closeness so that we could understand the fear of the Israelites? Perhaps many of us share the belief of Matthias Lane, the archivist of Martha Cooley's recent novel, *The Archivist.* He notes that he found the God of his wife's Jewish faith "unacceptably proximate. The One I had known all my life was believable in direct proportion to the distance He took from all the particulars of my life; His force as well as my faith lay in this remove."

During the Advent season of 1997 I became aware in prayer of such a fear of God's closeness. I was reflecting on the desire for the coming of the Lord, which is expressed so strongly in the liturgical texts of the season. Did I really want the coming of the Lord? At first I thought that the question was about what is called the Second Coming, the consummation of the world as we know it. I was aware that cataclysmic events in the world would, most probably, accompany such a consummation. Did I still want the coming of the Lord? I told Jesus that I still believed that the coming of the Lord would be for our good in spite of all the havoc that probably would accompany it. Then the question turned into something much more personal. "Do you want me to come close to you?" I felt immediately that this could mean my death. Thoughts of my own mortality had been in my mind around that time, prompted by my annual physical. I had to pause. Did I really want the coming of the Lord? Did I really want that much intimacy? It took a bit longer to come to the answer, but finally I did say: "I want you to come close, even if it means my death because I believe that you want only my good." I wonder if the fear of God's closeness has to do with some kind of deep fear that it will mean our death.

Once I had a period of a few weeks when I seemed to be "in the flow," as it were, when I felt in the presence of God often during the day, when I was able to live in the moment and not worry about the past or the future. It was a particularly graced time of my life. But then it disappeared, and I did not hanker after it. Nor did I wonder why it left me or ask God to give it back to me. Some years later I began to reflect on this strange phenomenon, namely, that a wonderful experience of seeming union with God should have passed out of my life without a whimper of regret on my part. I have also listened to other people who have had rather profound and joyful experiences of the presence of God in prayer and soon after stopped praying and did not know why. Is there some deep resistance to such experiences of God's presence? I came to the conclusion that there is.

When we are aware of God's presence, we are at the same time made aware of the fact that we are not in control of our lives. One of the reasons for avoiding prayer written out by the woman mentioned earlier in this chapter is: "Prayer takes me into a place where I don't know the terrain or the way. I'm not in charge." Ultimately we are made aware that we are not God, that God alone is God. This may be the deepest reason why in the Bible death is associated with seeing God's face, why we are so reluctant to reflect on our own mortality in meaningful ways, and why the thought of death is so taboo in our culture (cf. the Pulitzer Prize-winning book, *The Denial of Death* by Ernest Becker). Death presents us with the final proof that we are not in control, that we are not God. To come close to God forces us to give up the illusion that we are ultimately in control of our lives and of our deaths. Thus to see God face to face can seem to threaten death.

In his book *Care of Mind, Care of Spirit,* Gerald May notes that people who pray regularly are often puzzled that they pull away from very positive experiences of God. He believes that such people are "struggling with the very existence of self-image in the face of close appreciation of the divine." Later he writes:

> Ironically, one may have great trouble praying after going through an especially beautiful, consoling experience. Such experiences often imply considerable unconscious threat to self-importance in spite of their overt beauty. One's reaction to this may sometimes be to turn away from prayer for a while, and one may be mystified as to the reason.

When we are in the presence of God, we see reality whole, as it were, and we are not the center of it. This can be deeply threatening to our self-image and arouse considerable anxiety. Perhaps the biblical stories of the fear of God's face reflect this human reality. We fear the very thing that we most deeply want, namely, union with God.

Another personal experience may serve to illustrate the link between closeness to God and the realization of one's finitude. A couple of years ago while I was provincial of the Jesuits of New England I spent almost the whole of my annual retreat reflecting and praying over these words of the servant song of Isaiah 42:

> Here is my servant, whom I uphold, my chosen, in whom my soul delights; I have put my spirit upon him; he will bring forth justice to the nations. He will not cry or lift up his voice, or make it heard in the street; a bruised reed he will not break, and a dimly burning wick he will not quench; he will faithfully bring forth justice. He will not grow faint or be crushed until he has established justice in the earth; and the coastlands wait for his teaching. Thus says God, the Lord, who created the heavens and stretched them out, who spread out the earth and what comes from it, who gives breath to the people upon it and spirit to those who walk in it: I am the Lord, I have called you in righteousness, I have taken you by the hand and kept you; I have given you as a covenant to the people, a light to the nations, to open the eyes that are blind, to bring out the prisoners from the dungeon, from the prison those who sit in darkness. I am the Lord, that is my name; my glory I give to no other, nor my praise to idols. See, the former things have come to pass, and new things I now declare; before they spring forth, I tell you of them. (Is 42:1–9)

During my prayer periods I heard these words as spoken to me. God wants me as a servant. But in the midst of the call of the servant, God twice says, in effect, "But remember that I alone am God." "Thus says God, the Lord, who created the heavens and stretched them out." "I am the Lord, that is my name; my glory I give to no other." God does not need this servant; God does not need any servant; God does not need me. God does, however, want this servant, and God does want me as a servant. One evening during the retreat while walking outside after supper the words came to me: "You could be dead now." I was in the mood of the week, so I broke out in a rather broad smile. It was true. I had had a bout with cancer of the vocal cord, which could have killed me. In fact, my first cousin was at that moment dying of the same cancer. I could have been dead then, or dying, and the world would have gone on. Someone would be provincial and the province would carry on without my "leadership." It was a moment of grace and of happiness, and I keep praying that it will not leave me as completely as did the experience of being in the flow. In my most recent retreat I had an experience that taught me that I am still skittish in the presence of God, but perhaps more open. As I sat outside praying, a doe walked out of the woods. She stood there staring at me, pawing the ground, moving toward and away from me and the path she had been on. After about five minutes she seemed to become less frightened, and then with two snorts bounded off in the direction in which she had been heading. I thought with a smile that she was the image of me in the presence of God. Fortunately, I was able to talk about this image with God.

It is not easy, however, to keep the truth of the earlier retreat before my eyes. I want to be needed; in fact, I sometimes feel that I am not of use to others and cannot be loved unless I am needed by them. The experience of God destroys that illusion. With God I am, for sure, not needed.

But I am wanted, both as an intimate friend and as a servant of God's dream in this world. We can, however, easily
understand how threatening it is to realize that one's existence on this planet is so precarious that it depends not on
necessity but on God's desire and love alone.

Thus, one source of the dread of God's closeness is our
deep-seated delusion that we are self-sufficient and
immortal. To come close to God bursts the bubble of that
delusion. In addition, there is probably a deep-seated fear
that in coming close to God, in surrendering ourselves to
God, we will lose ourselves. The woman cited earlier in the
chapter wrote: "Prayer is a death, a letting go. Self-preser-
vation is the strongest of instincts. The milieu of faith and
God's world is not my natural habitat. I'm like a fish out of
water and that can be stood for a short time only and not
willingly (or eagerly) repeated. At the same time that's
where I want to be always." So what we most want also terrifies us. It is, however, paradoxically true that the more
we are united with God the more ourselves we are.

Because we see reality in the round when we are aware
of the presence of God, the experience of the divine is the
ground of humility. The fear we experience is, therefore,
salutary. "The fear of the Lord is the beginning of knowledge; fools despise wisdom and instruction" (Prv 1:7).
"The fear of the Lord is the beginning of wisdom; all those
who practice it have a good understanding" (Ps 111:10).
These are only two scriptural texts that enjoin on all
believers fear of God. In fact, in the Bible a frequent
response to the near presence of the divine is awe. Before
the burning bush, "Moses hid his face, for he was afraid to
look at God" (Ex 3:6). In Ezekiel we read: "So I rose up
and went out into the valley; and the glory of the Lord
stood there, like the glory that I had seen by the river
Chebar; and I fell on my face" (Ez 3:23). We might be

tempted to think that such fear would keep us from wanting intimacy with God. Yet the opposite seems to be true.

The experience of the divine includes more than dread as Rudolph Otto showed in his classic, *The Idea of the Holy.* Along with dread we find ourselves attracted to the "Wholly Other." Otto says that the "Holy" is a *mysterium tremendum et fascinans,* a mystery which evokes holy awe *(tremendum)* but which also fascinates. The very God who awes us also draws us. The mystery we call God strongly attracts us. "My soul longs, indeed it faints for the courts of the Lord; my heart and my flesh sing for joy to the living God" (Ps 84:2). And when God draws close in the scriptures, we often hear the words, "Fear not." When Gideon cries out in fear, he hears, "Peace be to you; do not fear, you shall not die" (Jgs 6:23). It is as if God wants to reassure us that this appropriate awe we feel is not the whole story. If we stay with the experience, God seems to say, we will find out that the nearness of the divine is for our bliss. The Book of Daniel describes a meeting with the Holy One:

> But then a hand touched me and roused me to my hands and knees. He said to me, "Daniel, greatly beloved, pay attention to the words that I am going to speak to you. Stand on your feet, for I have now been sent to you." So while he was speaking this word to me, I stood up trembling. He said to me, "Do not fear, Daniel, for from the first day that you set your mind to gain understanding and to humble yourself before your God, your words have been heard, and I have come because of your words...."
>
> While he was speaking these words to me, I turned my face toward the ground and was speechless. Then one in human form touched my lips, and I opened my mouth to speak, and said to the one who stood before me, "My lord, because of the vision such pains have

come upon me that I retain no strength. How can my
lord's servant talk with my lord? For I am shaking, no
strength remains in me, and no breath is left in me."
Again one in human form touched me and strengthened me. He said, "Do not fear, greatly beloved, you
are safe. Be strong and courageous!" When he spoke
to me, I was strengthened and said, "Let my lord
speak, for you have strengthened me." (Dn 10:11–19)

In this passage we can feel both the dread and the attrac-
tiveness of the divine. God speaks words of such tenderness that Daniel must be enraptured: "Daniel, greatly
beloved." As we read these words, do we not wish that we
could hear such words spoken directly to us? If we can
sense anything like such a sentiment, then we realize how
attractive God is.

Often in the scriptures fear of God is closely identified
with love of God. For example, in Deuteronomy Moses
presents the commandments to the people in these words:

Now this is the commandment—the statutes and the
ordinances—that the Lord your God charged me to
teach you to observe in the land that you are about to
cross into and occupy, so that you and your children
and your children's children may fear the Lord your
God all the days of your life, and keep all his decrees
and his commandments that I am commanding you,
so that your days may be long. Hear therefore, O
Israel, and observe them diligently, so that it may go
well with you, and so that you may multiply greatly
in a land flowing with milk and honey, as the Lord,
the God of your ancestors, has promised you. Hear, O
Israel: The Lord is our God, the Lord alone. You shall
love the Lord your God with all your heart, and with
all your soul, and with all your might. Keep these

words that I am commanding you today in your heart. Recite them to your children and talk about them when you are at home and when you are away, when you lie down and when you rise. Bind them as a sign on your hand, fix them as an emblem on your forehead, and write them on the doorposts of your house and on your gates. (Dt 6:1–9)

The pious Jew is drawn to God as a bee to honey. Fear of God, love of God and delight in God are intertwined. Of the promised shoot from the stump of Jesse, Isaiah writes: "The spirit of the Lord shall rest on him, the spirit of wisdom and understanding, the spirit of counsel and might, the spirit of knowledge and the fear of the Lord. His delight shall be in the fear of the Lord" (Is 11:2–3).

Throughout history men and women have experienced the paradox of being in awe and in love with the mystery we call God. Closeness to the mystery brings with it the conviction of how fleeting and puny we human beings are. At the same time we feel an overwhelming sense of wholeness and well-being in this presence. Paradoxically at the very moment when we realize at the deepest level of our being how fragile our existence is, how unnecessary we are, we feel loved and cared for, safe and saved. We yearn for "we know not what," and will not be satisfied until we are with that mystery. When we are aware of such moments, we want to sing. Perhaps at such a time of heightened awareness St. Alphonsus wrote the hymn translated as "O God of loveliness."

Our experience tells us that the closer we are to God the better off we are. But in spite of the evidence, we still back away as from a precipice from allowing God to fulfill our deepest desire. We need to beg God to help us to overcome this fear, which keeps us from what is for our peace. One day when I was praying about the topic of this chapter it

occurred to me that the deepest meaning of the fairy tale
of *Beauty and the Beast* may have to do with the fear of the
human heart before God. God, like the Beast, wants us to
know him as love, but we, like Beauty, are terrified by his
size and what seems to us his fury. If we allow God to come
close, if we kiss the Beast, we will find that he is only love
and delights in us and in our love.

A prayer of St. Teresa of Avila expresses the desire and
hints at the ambivalence of that desire:

> If, Lord, Thy love for me is strong
> As this which binds me unto Thee,
> What holds me from Thee, Lord, so long,
> What holds Thee, Lord, so long from me?
> O soul, what then desirest thou?
> —Lord, I would see, who thus choose Thee.
> What fears can yet assail thee now?
> —All that I fear is to lose Thee.
> Love's whole possession I entreat,
> Lord, make my soul Thine own abode,
> And I will build a nest so sweet
> It may not be too poor for God.
> O soul in God hidden from sin,
> What more desires for thee remain,
> Save but to love, and love again,
> And all on flame with love within,
> Love on, and turn to love again?

Chapter 5

Hearts in Hiding

The fear of God's face arises from the nature of who God is and who we are. We are appropriately afraid before the mystery we call God, and God, it seems, tries to do everything possible to attract us and to reassure us that ultimately we have nothing to fear from closeness. But there is another kind of fear that is a close relative to the kind of shame and fear we experience when we have offended a good friend. Will she still love me, be my friend, now that I have betrayed her trust? Before God all of us realize that we have fallen short, that we have not lived up to the moral integrity required in this relationship. In this chapter we will explore the disturbance in the relationship that comes with the consciousness of being a sinner before God. What is God's reaction to my sinning? How do I act in the relationship when I am aware that I have fallen "short of the glory of God" (Rom 3:23)?

Once I met a woman who said that she could not read the Bible. Whenever she tried, all she found were condemnations that depressed her. My initial reaction was to wonder why she missed so much else in the Bible. There is no question, however, that she could find a number of passages where God angrily condemns individuals and a whole people for their sinfulness and infidelity. Here are a few examples:

> The Lord rejected all the descendants of Israel; he punished them and gave them into the hand of plunderers, until he had banished them from his presence. (2 Kgs 17:20)
>
> Indeed, Jerusalem and Judah so angered the Lord that he expelled them from his presence. (2 Kgs 24:20)

Parts of the Book of Leviticus reek with condemnations and assurances that the Lord will turn his face away from evildoers. In the Book of Deuteronomy Moses is told to write a song to remind the Israelites of who God is and to warn them against idolatry and apostasy. One of the warnings is chilling:

> Jacob ate his fill; Jeshurun grew fat, and kicked. You grew fat, bloated, and gorged! He abandoned God who made him, and scoffed at the Rock of his salvation. They made him jealous with strange gods, with abhorrent things they provoked him. They sacrificed to demons, not God, to deities they had never known, to new ones recently arrived, whom your ancestors had not feared. You were unmindful of the Rock that bore you; you forgot the God who gave you birth.
>
> The Lord saw it, and was jealous; he spurned his sons and daughters. He said: I will hide my face from them, I will see what their end will be; for they are a perverse generation, children in whom there is no faithfulness. They made me jealous with what is no god, provoked me with their idols. So I will make them jealous with what is no people, provoke them

with a foolish nation. For a fire is kindled by my anger, and burns to the depths of Sheol; it devours the earth and its increase, and sets on fire the foundations of the mountains. I will heap disasters upon them, spend my arrows against them: wasting hunger, burning consumption, bitter pestilence. The teeth of beasts I will send against them, with venom of things crawling in the dust. (Dt 32:15 –24)

If the woman I met kept meeting such passages when she opened the Bible, her reaction makes some sense. Even if we are not troubled by excessive guilt and a very poor self-image, as this woman probably was, we can find passages such as these daunting. After all, none of us can honestly say that we have not offended God. Will we find the divine face turned away from us in anger and condemnation?

Many of us were brought up feeling that God was like a bloodhound on the trail of sins of all kinds. We can resonate with what the writer Jon Hassler said of his experience in Catholic school before Sister Constance said that children served God by playing. "As third-graders, we'd been struggling so hard to memorize the catechism, pray five times a day, and refrain from eating or drinking before Communion that we were led to believe that being good was like picking your way through a minefield." Hence the reaction of the woman who could not read the Bible is understandable; sad, but understandable. Such an image of God would tend to keep anyone distant. After all, I would not want to approach someone who had been a close friend and whom I had offended if I expected nothing but rejection and condemnation. In fact, this must have been the expectation of the woman I met. Hence she stayed as far away from the Bible and, I presume, from God as she could.

These texts of scripture, however, do not exhaust the

revelation of God's attitude toward sinners. In one passage we read not only of the wrath of the Lord, but also of a change of heart.

> In overflowing wrath for a moment I hid my face from you, but with everlasting love I will have compassion on you, says the Lord, your Redeemer. This is like the days of Noah to me: Just as I swore that the waters of Noah would never again go over the earth, so I have sworn that I will not be angry with you and will not rebuke you. For the mountains may depart and the hills be removed, but my steadfast love shall not depart from you, and my covenant of peace shall not be removed, says the Lord, who has compassion on you. (Is 54:8–10)

Over and over again in the Hebrew Bible Yahweh is depicted as a compassionate and forgiving God. In the days of the wicked kings after Solomon, Israel was beset on all sides, and the calamities were considered punishment for the sins of idolatry of the kings and people. Yet after Elisha died, we read: "Now King Hazael of Aram oppressed Israel all the days of Jehoahaz. But the Lord was gracious to them and had compassion on them; he turned toward them, because of his covenant with Abraham, Isaac, and Jacob, and would not destroy them; nor has he banished them from his presence until now" (2 Kgs 13:22–23). Though the people betray the covenant, Yahweh does not renounce them as would be expected on the basis of the analogy of a covenant between a more powerful king and a vassal. A powerful king would destroy a vassal who had betrayed the covenant.

Instead, in the Hebrew Bible Yahweh is depicted as going to great lengths to bring the people back to intimacy. The Book of Hosea is a remarkable account of such lengths. The conceit behind the book is that Hosea marries a harlot and does everything he can to win the love of this continually wayward woman. After describing the infidelity of the woman, who is the symbol of Israel, the prophet speaks in Yahweh's name:

> Therefore, I will now allure her, and bring her into the wilderness, and speak tenderly to her. From there I will give her her vineyards, and make the Valley of Achor a door of hope. There she shall respond as in the days of her youth, as at the time when she came out of the land of Egypt. On that day, says the Lord, you will call me, "My husband," and no longer will you call me, "My Baal." For I will remove the names of the Baals from her mouth, and they shall be mentioned by name no more. I will make for you a covenant on that day with the wild animals, the birds of the air, and the creeping things of the ground; and I will abolish the bow, the sword, and war from the land; and I will make you lie down in safety. And I will take you for my wife forever; I will take you for my wife in righteousness and in justice, in steadfast love, and in mercy. I will take you for my wife in faithfulness; and you shall know the Lord. (Hos 2:14–20)

Samuel Terrien notes that Hosea finds "in his own emotional upheaval the mirror of divine pathos....Repentance is the response to gratuitous love, not its condition." In other words, Hosea believes that Yahweh's heart is broken, not enraged, by the infidelity of the people. God hopes that unconditional, gratuitous forgiveness and love will win them back as Hosea hoped to win back the love of his wife, Gomer. God does not wait until we repent to show us gratuitous love. God's desire for intimacy with us is that strong.

The lengths to which Yahweh will go to win back a sinful people are again evident in the complaints Micah puts in his mouth, complaints that are the model for the "Reproaches" sung during the adoration of the cross in the Good Friday liturgy:

> Hear what the Lord says: Rise, plead your case before the mountains, and let the hills hear your voice. Hear, you mountains, the controversy of the Lord, and you enduring foundations of the earth; for the Lord has a controversy with his people, and he will contend with Israel. "O my people, what have I done to you? In what have I wearied you? Answer me! For I brought you up from the land of Egypt, and redeemed you from the house of slavery; and I sent before you Moses, Aaron, and Miriam. O my people, remember now what King Balak of Moab devised, what Balaam son of Beor answered him, and what happened from Shittim to Gilgal, that you may know the saving acts of the Lord." (Mi 6:1–5)

The creator of the universe abases himself before Israel, asking them to explain why they have turned away and begging them to return. Is this a God who terrifies? Once again we meet the One who will do everything possible, including demeaning himself, to win over people to a relationship of intimacy. Even infidelity, idolatry and apostasy do not derail the divine desire and dream.

Jesus' parable of the prodigal son expresses poignantly indeed God's love for the wayward sinner and for a wayward people. Even without an understanding of the culture of Jesus' time and audience this parable is a powerful expression of God's love and forgiveness. But I found that it made an even stronger impact when I discovered some of the cultural background. In the peasant society in which Jesus told the story the younger son would, in effect, be telling his father "I want you dead" when he asks for his inheritance. His father would be expected to beat him to within an inch of his life for such impiety. Instead, the father does what the son wants and thus allows the son to waste his inheritance on wanton living. Jesus' hearers would already be stunned at the liberality of the father and would already probably get the picture that this is the way God has related with them over and over again. I am reminded of the fifth point in Ignatius's meditation on personal sins. After the person has come to a knowledge of all his or her sins in the presence of God, the fifth point is:

> This is an exclamation of wonder and surging emotion, uttered as I reflect on all creatures and wonder how they have allowed me to live and have preserved me in life. The angels: How is it that, although they are swords of God's justice, they have borne with me, protected me, and prayed for me? The saints: How is it that they have interceded and prayed for me? Likewise, the heavens, the sun, the moon, the stars, and the elements; the fruits, birds, fishes, and animals. And the earth: How is it that it has not opened up and swallowed me, creating new hells for me to suffer in forever?

A peasant hearing Jesus tell the story of the father who actually gave his son his inheritance after such an insulting request might well feel the emotions Ignatius describes. When the son leaves the village, he would leave in disgrace, and everyone in the village would know it. They would also hear about how he had defiled himself by hiring himself out to a pagan to take care of his pigs, animals that are particularly unclean to a Jew. When the disgraced son comes to his senses and returns, what do the

villagers see? They see a father who does the unthinkable
again, demeaning himself further. When he sees his son at
a distance, he slips off his sandals, hikes up his garments
and runs barefoot through the village to throw his arms
around the wastrel. Moreover, he throws a party to which
the whole village is invited. He treats the older son with
similar compassion and love. The elder son's attitude and
remarks are almost as insulting to the father as were those
of the younger son. He, too, in effect tells the father that he
wishes him dead. Instead of rejecting his son, the father
says: "Son, you are always with me, and all that is mine is
yours. But we had to celebrate and rejoice, because this
brother of yours was dead and has come to life; he was lost
and has been found" (Lk 15:31–32). (For a moving meditation on Rembrandt's painting see Henri Nouwen's *The
Return of the Prodigal Son.*)

This parable may not, in the first place, refer to the forgiveness of the individual sinner. In *Jesus and the Victory of
God* N. T. Wright makes a strong case that Jesus here is
telling the story of Israel in the light of his own understanding of his ministry. Historically Israel has many times
told God to get lost, to drop dead. They have trusted in foreign alliances and in foreign gods, and have paid the
price. They, too, have become slaves to foreigners and
have defiled themselves. God has given them the freedom
and ability to do so. Yet each time when Israel has come to
her senses and returned, she has found God prodigal with
love and forgiveness. Also, when the exiles came back
from Babylon, those Israelites and Samaritans who had
remained on the land acted like the older brother in the
parable. They resented the returnees and God's reception
of them. Wright believes that Jesus is pointedly telling his
opponents that they are like the Samaritans and others
who resented the Israelites who returned from exile and
were welcomed by Yahweh. It is good for us who have

imbibed individualism almost with our mother's milk to be reminded that God's love is a tent that covers all creation and invites all to join the party under the tent. Jesus, who welcomes tax collectors, sinners, prostitutes, lepers and the poor to his companionship, likens those who resent such easy welcome to the elder brother and to those who remained on the land during the exile. Let those who have ears to hear, hear.

Of course, the ultimate proof of the divine compassion and forgiveness is given to us on the cross at Golgotha. Human beings cruelly torture and kill God's own son, the greatest proof of God's desire for intimacy with us, and what happens? Here, if ever it were to happen, one would expect the final repudiation of the divine dream and desire. But instead we hear: "Father, forgive them; for they do not know what they are doing" (Lk 23:34). A scene in Tolkien's *The Fellowship of the Ring* gives an inkling of what we experience when we contemplate Jesus dying cruelly at Golgotha. The companions who make up the fellowship have come into the forest of the elves. Dwarfs and elves deeply distrust one another. One of the group, the dwarf Gimli looks into the eyes of Galadriel, the elf queen, who has just spoken of the fabled lands of the dwarfs in the dwarf language.

> She [Galadriel] looked upon Gimli, who sat glowering and sad, and she smiled. And the Dwarf, hearing the names given in his own ancient tongue, looked up and met her eyes; and it seemed to him that he looked suddenly into the heart of an enemy and saw there love and understanding. Wonder came into his face, and then he smiled in answer.

When we look into the eyes of Jesus dying on the cross at the hands of human beings like us, we too look into the eyes of one who, we fear, is an enemy now, but there find love and forgiveness.

With this example we are at the point of examining the stance of the sinner before God. As noted earlier, when we have offended or betrayed a friend in some way, our initial reaction is to want to avoid his or her presence. We withdraw from intimacy. That is also our way with the Lord. We are afraid, and like Adam and Eve, we hide. If we are to believe the Bible, the Lord will not let us stay in hiding. Just as Yahweh continued to walk in the garden and called Adam and Eve out of their hiding, so too the Lord continues to try to draw us out of hiding.

To leave our hiding place, however, is not easy. We are, first of all, afraid of the punishment we will receive. But, in addition, to leave our hiding place means to change our style of life. To return to an intimate relationship with the Lord we must turn away from those ways of thinking and acting that have disrupted the relationship. "Turn to me and be saved, all the ends of the earth! For I am God, and there is no other. By myself I have sworn, from my mouth has gone forth in righteousness a word that shall not return: 'To me every knee shall bow, every tongue shall swear'" (Is 45:22–23). God has not changed to disrupt the relationship; we have. When I sin, I choose to do something that disrupts the Peaceable Kingdom or at least my part of it, the dream of God for me and for my world. We need to look more closely at the disruption of sin in order to understand better the nature of the disruption that has occurred.

When Moses gave the Israelites the commandments, he explained that Yahweh was offering them a choice between life and death:

> See, I have set before you today life and prosperity, death and adversity. If you obey the commandments of the Lord your God that I am commanding you

today, by loving the Lord your God, walking in his ways, and observing his commandments, decrees, and ordinances, then you shall live and become numerous, and the Lord your God will bless you in the land that you are entering to possess. But if your heart turns away and you do not hear, but are led astray to bow down to other gods and serve them, I declare to you today that you shall perish; you shall not live long in the land that you are crossing the Jordan to enter and possess. I call heaven and earth to witness against you today that I have set before you life and death, blessings and curses. Choose life so that you and your descendants may live, loving the Lord your God, obeying him, and holding fast to him; for that means life to you and length of days, so that you may live in the land that the Lord swore to give to your ancestors, to Abraham, to Isaac, and to Jacob. (Dt 30:15–20)

This sounds like a dire warning, and it is, but it does not come to the Israelites as a despot's willful and arbitrary demand for blind obedience. What is at stake for the Israelites, individually and corporately, is their very identity; they are a people holy to the Lord. This is their glory and their joy. If they turn away from this identity, then they will surely die. But life and death here do not refer only to physical life or death, or even to their life or death as a distinct people. "'Life' here is not only physical existence, it means also life in proximity to the Lord, whose very presence means security and *shalom*, 'peace.' With this nuance, the word 'life' and its opposite, 'death,' often occur in liturgical texts for presence or absence of the Lord" (Richard Clifford, *Deuteronomy*). Sin, in other words, will not be a matter of breaking a commandment imposed arbitrarily; it will mean going against their own deepest good, the desire of their hearts. For this reason the psalmist can declare: "Happy are those whose way is blameless, who walk in the law of the Lord. Happy are those who keep his decrees, who seek him with their whole heart, who also do no wrong, but walk in his ways" (Ps 119:1–3). This psalm, the longest by far in the psalter, is one long paean to the beauties of the Law of the Lord.

Sin means turning away from God. Our behavior betrays this, I believe. If I have offended a close friend or done something that I believe she would not approve, I do not feel right in her presence, even if she does not (yet) know what I have done. I become more reserved in speaking with her; I am not as forthcoming about my deepest feelings and thoughts because the matter between us continually intrudes. In other words, I am hiding from her. But I am also not happy in the friendship as I once was, and I wonder how to get over the barrier that my behavior has set up. When I have acted against my conscience, I act the same way with God. I tend to avoid prayer, to keep what prayer I do on a somewhat superficial level. Like Adam and Eve I go into hiding. But as in the case of my good friend, hiding does not make me happy. Just as the only way to move forward in the relationship with my friend is to address the issue between us directly, so too with the Lord.

What happens when I do speak openly with my friend about my offensive behavior and its consequences? If the friendship has a solid wall and a sure foundation, then I find forgiveness and renewed friendship. I may also find out that my hiding had been bugging her; that she had not understood why I was so distant in recent times. I may find that she is more angry at this distance, which betrays a lack of trust in the friendship than in the offensive behavior itself. I have noticed that God's anger in the Hebrew Bible seems to be reserved for those who do not acknowledge their offenses. For example:

But my people have forgotten me, they burn offerings to a delusion; they have stumbled in their ways, in the ancient roads, and have gone into bypaths, not the highway, making their land a horror, a thing to be hissed at forever. All who pass by it are horrified and shake their heads. Like the wind from the east, I will scatter them before the enemy. I will show them my back, not my face, in the day of their calamity. (Jer 18:15–17)

Or again:

I was ready to be sought out by those who did not ask, to be found by those who did not seek me. I said, "Here I am, here I am," to a nation that did not call on my name. I held out my hands all day long to a rebellious people, who walk in a way that is not good, following their own devices; a people who provoke me to my face continually, sacrificing in gardens and offering incense on bricks; who sit inside tombs, and spend the night in secret places; who eat swine's flesh, with broth of abominable things in their vessels; who say, "Keep to yourself, do not come near me, for I am too holy for you." These are a smoke in my nostrils, a fire that burns all day long. See, it is written before me: I will not keep silent, but I will repay; I will indeed repay into their laps their iniquities and their ancestors' iniquities together, says the Lord; because they offered incense on the mountains and reviled me on the hills, I will measure into their laps full payment for their actions. (Is 65:1–7)

In this passage it is clear that the Lord wants to draw this people into his embrace, wants to forgive, but their hard-heartedness prevents this.

If, however, the people turn to God and confess their sins, the reaction is not anger, but forgiveness and, in some instances, overwhelming tenderness. For example, after Solomon finished building the temple

> ...the Lord appeared to Solomon in the night and said to him: "I have heard your prayer, and have chosen this place for myself as a house of sacrifice. When I shut up the heavens so that there is no rain, or command the locust to devour the land, or send pestilence among my people, if my people who are called by my name humble themselves, pray, seek my face, and turn from their wicked ways, then I will hear from heaven, and will forgive their sin and heal their land. Now my eyes will be open and my ears attentive to the prayer that is made in this place." (2 Chr 7:12–15)

The whole prophecy of Hosea with its parable of Hosea's love of his harlot wife demonstrates the divine compassion and willingness to forgive and shows the Lord as almost desperate to convince the people of his tender love.

When the prodigal son comes to his senses and turns back to his father's house, the father runs out to him and throws his arms around him in joy. In the gospels Jesus' anger, for the most part, is reserved for those who are unwilling to admit their need for forgiveness. For example, he inveighs against the Pharisees:

> "Woe to you, scribes and Pharisees, hypocrites! For you clean the outside of the cup and of the plate, but inside they are full of greed and self-indulgence. You blind Pharisee! First clean the inside of the cup, so that the outside also may become clean.

"Woe to you, scribes and Pharisees, hypocrites! For you are like whitewashed tombs, which on the outside look beautiful, but inside they are full of the bones of the dead and of all kinds of filth. So you also on the outside look righteous to others, but inside you are full of hypocrisy and lawlessness." (Mt 23:25–28)

Jesus told the parable of the Pharisee and the tax collector "to some who trusted in themselves that they were righteous and regarded others with contempt."

"Two men went up to the temple to pray, one a Pharisee and the other a tax collector. The Pharisee, standing by himself, was praying thus, 'God, I thank you that I am not like other people: thieves, rogues, adulterers, or even like this tax collector. I fast twice a week; I give a tenth of all my income.' But the tax collector, standing far off, would not even look up to heaven, but was beating his breast and saying, 'God, be merciful to me, a sinner!' I tell you, this man went down to his home justified rather than the other; for all who exalt themselves will be humbled, but all who humble themselves will be exalted." (Lk 18:10–14)

In addition, Jesus was known and, indeed, chastised for sharing meals with tax collectors and sinners. Tax collectors were disliked, at least in Galilee, because they were considered dishonest, men who charged more than was required and kept the extra for themselves. And "sinners" are not the "likes of us," but rather people who are actually irreligious. According to John Meier in *A Marginal Jew:*

Sinners were those who intentionally rejected the commandments of the God of Israel, as these commandments were understood by Jews in general, not just by an elite group of puritans. Jesus' table fellowship was therefore seriously offensive to many Jews, not just to...Pharisees. He insisted on entering into intimate relationship not only with dishonest Jews who robbed their fellows (the tax collectors) but also with those Jews who, for all practical purposes, had thumbed their noses at the covenant and commandments of God. It was to these wicked that Jesus dared to offer forgiveness and a place in the kingdom of God, without apparently making it a prior condition that they go through the usual process of reintegration into Jewish religious society: prayers of repentance, restitution of ill-gotten goods or recompense for harm committed, temple sacrifice, and commitment to following the Mosaic Law. His bon vivant existence with robbers and sinners was therefore something much more scandalous and ominous than a mere matter of breaking purity rules dear to the...Pharisees.

There is, obviously, no need to be afraid to appear before Jesus to confess one's sins.

The way to restore the friendship we have broken by our sins is by getting back into the relationship in whatever way we can. For some it might come through such a prayer as was made by Ezra:

At the evening sacrifice I got up from my fasting, with my garments and my mantle torn, and fell on my knees, spread out my hands to the Lord my God, and said, "O my God, I am too ashamed and embarrassed to lift my face to you, my God, for our iniquities have risen higher than our heads, and our guilt has mounted up to the heavens. From the days of our ancestors to this day we have been deep in guilt, and for our iniquities we, our kings, and our priests have been handed over to the kings of the lands, to the sword, to captivity, to plundering, and to utter shame, as is now the case. But now for a brief moment favor has been shown by the Lord our God, who has left us a remnant, and given us a stake in his holy place, in order that he may brighten our eyes and grant us a little sustenance in our slavery. For we are slaves; yet our God has not forsaken us in our slavery, but has extended to us his steadfast love before the kings of Persia, to give us new life to set up the house of our God, to repair its ruins, and to give us a wall in Judea and Jerusalem." (Ezr 9:5–9)

For others it may come through contemplating some of the scenes of the gospels where Jesus is shown as hobnobbing with sinners. For example, does Jesus ask me three times "Do you love me?" as he did to Peter? Can I look him in the eyes as he hangs on the cross? Can I ask him to take me back into his friendship? The only way we can continue to offend God and remain estranged is to persist in hiding.

Finally let's return to the issue of God's anger at sinners. Just as parents are angry at children who hurt themselves by their actions, so too, it is possible that God can be angry with us, who so persistently act against our own and the world's best interests. The scriptures ascribe the emotions of anger, sadness, grief and tender love to God. It is, of course, possible that we project such emotions onto the mystery we call God. That is, our sins make us feel alienated from God, and we expect that he will be angry. The parable of the prodigal son may reveal Jesus' deepest understanding of God as one who is never angry. Julian of Norwich more than once asserts that in God there is no wrath or anger. Still the Israelites and the early Christians seem to have concluded that God is revealed as who he is through stories of passionate interchange with human beings. We can note, moreover, that in the scriptures the divine anger seems to intend our conversion, a return to the intimacy that has been disrupted by our sins. It is the kind of anger that reveals deep love and concern. Indeed, it seems in Hosea and other prophets to be a sorrowful anger. And it is an anger that can be deflected through the intercession of intimate friends such as Abraham or Moses. After the Israelites had made the golden calf while Moses was on the mountain, God's anger is depicted as blazing hot and bent on destruction:

> But Moses implored the Lord his God, and said, "O Lord, why does your wrath burn hot against your people, whom you brought out of the land of Egypt with great power and with a mighty hand? Why should the Egyptians say, 'It was with evil intent that he brought them out to kill them in the mountains, and to consume them from the face of the earth'? Turn from your fierce wrath; change your mind and do not bring disaster on your people. Remember Abraham, Isaac, and Israel, your servants, how you swore to them by your own self, saying to them, 'I will multiply your descendants like the stars of heaven, and all this land that I have promised I will give to your descendants, and they shall inherit it forever.'" And the Lord changed his mind about the disaster that he planned to bring on his people. (Ex 32:11–14)

The Lord, even when white hot with anger, does not want to destroy but to bring about a conversion of heart.

This may be a good place to bring in the notion of the discernment of spirits. When we experience movements of our hearts in relation to God and to our lives, we have to decide which of them are from God and which are not. St. Ignatius gives us some good rules of thumb in the *Spiritual Exercises.* To my mind, the most important are the first two, where Ignatius begins from the basic orientation of a person's life.

> *The First Rule.* In the case of persons who are going from one mortal sin to another, the enemy ordinarily proposes to them apparent pleasures. He makes them imagine delights and pleasures of the senses, in order to hold them fast and plunge them deeper into their sins and vices.
>
> But with persons of this type the good spirit uses a contrary procedure. Through their good judgment on problems of morality he stings their consciences with remorse.
>
> *The Second.* In the cases of persons who are earnestly purging away their sins, and who are progressing from good to better in the service of God our Lord, the procedure used is the opposite of that described in the First Rule. For in this case it is characteristic of the evil spirit to cause gnawing anxiety, to sadden, and to set up obstacles. In this way he unsettles these persons by false reasons aimed at preventing their progress.
>
> But with persons of this type it is characteristic of the good spirit to stir up courage and strength, consolations, tears, inspirations, and tranquility. He makes things easier and eliminates all obstacles, so that the persons may move forward in doing good.

When we are estranged from God, we will experience pricks of conscience, feelings of being out of sorts and perhaps a sense that the Lord is angry with us. The purpose of these movements is to bring us back to our senses, to bring us back to the relationship of intimacy with the Lord. On the other hand, the voices that tempt us will try to soothe us, to make us believe that we are OK. But when we are on the right path, then the movements that trouble do not ordinarily come from the Lord, who wants us to enjoy intimacy with him; they will emanate from the evil one or from that part of us that shrinks from the awe-filled realization that we are not the center of the universe. Again we note that the divine anger is aimed at conversion, not destruction. The Lord has our best interests at heart.

After a talk on intimacy with God I was asked about the existence of hell. How can we square the existence of hell with the last statement, namely, that the Lord has our best interests at heart? The only answer I could give is this: God cannot force anyone to opt for intimacy. One of the fearsome risks of creation is that those who are created will refuse the offer of intimacy, and refuse it absolutely and irrevocably. I thought of parents who bring a child into the world; they have no guarantee that the child will love them for doing so, that the child will not hate them for bringing him or her into this world. God takes that risk in creating free persons; they may refuse to accept the invitation to union with the Trinity. That refusal, if it is irrevocable, is hell. How does God react to such a refusal? I am reminded of a story told by a rabbi of the Middle Ages. It seems that when the Egyptians were destroyed at the Red Sea, there was great rejoicing in heaven. But they noticed that God was weeping. "Why are you weeping when you have won such a great victory for your people?" asked one of the angels. "The Egyptians are also my people," he replied. The teller of this story discerned something very true of our God. If one of God's beloved people does choose defiance and alienation irrevocably, I can imagine God weeping.

Chapter 6

Anger and Intimacy with God

We have just noted that divine anger at sinners can be understood as motivated by tender mercy and love for them. Hence it expresses God's continuing love and desire for intimacy. What about our expression of anger at God? Does that show our love and friendship with God?

The road to intimacy in any relationship is never a smooth and easy one. Our fears, anxieties and sensitivities put potholes in it, for one thing. Few of us are so self-confident that we can approach a new relationship without such feelings. In addition, we approach any new relationship with psychological baggage that makes it difficult to see the new person as he or she really is. For example, a new friend reminds me of my brother, with whom I have a strong love-hate relationship. He makes an innocent remark that offends me because it triggers feelings that have to do with my brother. To complicate matters my new friend also carries psychological baggage into our relationship. So even with the best of intentions on both sides there will be times when the relationship is disrupted by anger and resentment toward one another. And then there are times when my friend angers me by doing something without the best of intentions; for example, because of selfishness he lets me down when I had been counting on him. In any relationship there will be times when we have a bumpy ride because of anger and resentment toward each other.

When we experience such anger and resentment toward a friend, we often experience anxiety; I wonder whether I made a mistake in trusting her, whether she will drop me if I express my outrage at her actions, whether I really want to maintain the friendship. Some people retreat into silence when angered by a friend; thus they retreat from the openness that had been a hallmark of the friendship. Some can only express anger indirectly, through actions that are called passive-aggressive. Some blow up and figure that the friendship is over. When these and like behaviors take over in a relationship, then one of the two friends has gone into hiding. The relationship of intimacy is, indeed, threatened. Note, however, that it is not threatened by the anger itself, but by the retreat from openness and honesty. If, as the poet Seamus Heaney says, the two have built the wall of their friendship well enough, then they need not fear; there may be some difficulties ahead, but they can negotiate them because they can communicate honestly their angers, resentments and hurt.

The greatest difficulty, of course, both for a human relationship and for the relationship with God comes for those who have not built the wall of friendship well. There are people who, because of traumata suffered in life, find it hard to trust others, including the Author of life. The woman who could not open the Bible without experiencing condemnation comes to mind. I have also met people who have been so hurt by life that they find it very difficult to trust life or its Author. Words such as those of the Book of Wisdom's "You spare all things, for they are yours, O Lord, you who love the living" (Wis 11:26) often ring hollow or mean nothing to people who have been abused as

children or who have suffered debilitating physical or psychiatric illnesses in the prime of life. It takes a great deal of
patient pastoral care for such people to experience a God
whom they can trust.

But it is possible. After a talk on prayer as a personal
relationship a woman spoke about her experience of having been sexually abused by her father. For a long time she
had wondered where God was while she suffered. She had
learned to express her anger at and mistrust of God with
the help of some good pastoral care. Finally she realized in
prayer that God had suffered with her, had wept with her,
and still had compassion for her. This experience had
made the difference that helped her to develop a life of
intimacy with God and with others. I have met people
with debilitating feelings of self-doubt and scrupulosity
who have, with patient pastoral care, discovered that they
could trust God. (In *What Do I Want in Prayer?* I have provided some exercises that might help people who have
trouble trusting God.)

In the Bible we find instances where people poured out
their hearts to God, even sometimes in real anger. For
example, though it ends positively, Psalm 13 may well
speak for many of us, at least some times in our lives.

> How long, O Lord? Will you forget me forever? How
> long will you hide your face from me? How long must
> I bear pain in my soul, and have sorrow in my heart
> all day long? How long shall my enemy be exalted
> over me? Consider and answer me, O Lord my God!
> Give light to my eyes, or I will sleep the sleep of death,
> and my enemy will say, "I have prevailed"; my foes
> will rejoice because I am shaken. But I trusted in your
> steadfast love; my heart shall rejoice in your salva-
> tion. I will sing to the Lord, because he has dealt
> bountifully with me.

Hannah, the wife of Elkanah, is another example. Her plight is described in the first chapter of the First Book of Samuel. She was childless while Elkanah's other wife had many children. Hannah suffered grievously every time that the family went up to Shiloh to worship and offer sacrifice. Elkanah tried to console her, but she remained inconsolable. In her anguish,

> Hannah rose and presented herself before the Lord. Now Eli the priest was sitting on the seat beside the doorpost of the temple of the Lord. She was deeply distressed and prayed to the Lord, and wept bitterly. She made this vow: "O Lord of hosts, if only you will look on the misery of your servant, and remember me, and not forget your servant, but will give to your servant a male child, then I will set him before you as a nazirite until the day of his death. He shall drink neither wine nor intoxicants, and no razor shall touch his head." As she continued praying before the Lord, Eli observed her mouth. Hannah was praying silently; only her lips moved, but her voice was not heard; therefore Eli thought she was drunk. So Eli said to her, "How long will you make a drunken spectacle of yourself? Put away your wine." But Hannah answered, "No, my lord, I am a woman deeply troubled; I have drunk neither wine nor strong drink, but I have been pouring out my soul before the Lord. Do not regard your servant as a worthless woman, for I have been speaking out of my great anxiety and vexation all this time." Then Eli answered, "Go in peace; the God of Israel grant the petition you have made to him." And she said, "Let your servant find favor in your sight." Then the woman went to her quarters, ate and drank with her husband, and her countenance was sad no longer. (1 Sm 1:9–18)

Hannah has poured out her heart and soul to the Lord and has gone home consoled.

The complaints of the psalmist and of Hannah are mild, indeed, compared to those of Jeremiah, the reluctant prophet at the time just before the Babylonian captivity. When he heard the call of God, he cried out: "Ah, Lord God! Truly I do not know how to speak, for I am only a boy" (Jer 1:6). More than likely Jeremiah knew what awaited him if he accepted the call to be a prophet. He did not want the job; indeed, it seems that he never really reconciled himself to it. "Woe is me, my mother, that you ever bore me, a man of strife and contention to the whole land! I have not lent, nor have I borrowed, yet all of them curse me" (Jer 15:10). He had to speak unpalatable truths to the leaders and the people who preferred the comforting words of the false prophets. His life was threatened; he was thrown into a cistern; even his family seems to have plotted against him. He lashed out in anger at his enemies, begging God in violent language to do them in. And he did not spare God from his anger.

> O Lord, you know; remember me and visit me, and bring down retribution for me on my persecutors. In your forbearance do not take me away; know that on your account I suffer insult. Your words were found, and I ate them, and your words became to me a joy and the delight of my heart; for I am called by your name, O Lord, God of hosts. I did not sit in the company of merrymakers, nor did I rejoice; under the weight of your hand I sat alone, for you had filled me with indignation. Why is my pain unceasing, my wound incurable, refusing to be healed? Truly, you are to me like a deceitful brook, like waters that fail. (Jer 15:15–18)

Earlier Jeremiah had called Yahweh "the fountain of living water" (Jer 2:13). Now in his agony he speaks almost blasphemously of God as failing him in his hour of need like a dry brook, a deceitful brook at that.

Jeremiah must have been tempted to give up his prophetic call as we hear in the following passage where he begins by calling God a seducer:

O Lord, you have enticed me, and I was enticed; you have overpowered me, and you have prevailed. I have become a laughingstock all day long; everyone mocks me. For whenever I speak, I must cry out, I must shout, "Violence and destruction!" For the word of the Lord has become for me a reproach and derision all day long. If I say, "I will not mention him, or speak any more in his name," then within me there is something like a burning fire shut up in my bones; I am weary with holding it in, and I cannot. For I hear many whispering: "Terror is all around! Denounce him! Let us denounce him!" All my close friends are watching for me to stumble. "Perhaps he can be enticed, and we can prevail against him, and take our revenge on him." But the Lord is with me like a dread warrior; therefore my persecutors will stumble, and they will not prevail. They will be greatly shamed, for they will not succeed. Their eternal dishonor will never be forgotten. O Lord of hosts, you test the righteous, you see the heart and the mind; let me see your retribution upon them, for to you I have committed my cause. Sing to the Lord; praise the Lord! For he has delivered the life of the needy from the hands of evildoers. (Jer 20:7–13)

Jeremiah not only can speak angrily about his enemies, but also can denounce God directly. He would prefer not to

speak the words of God, but he must. Speaking them, however, does him no good. The depth of his desperation and
depression are revealed in the words that follow immediately upon the passage just cited:

> Cursed be the day on which I was born! The day when
> my mother bore me, let it not be blessed! Cursed be
> the man who brought the news to my father, saying,
> "A child is born to you, a son," making him very glad.
> Let that man be like the cities that the Lord overthrew
> without pity; let him hear a cry in the morning and
> an alarm at noon, because he did not kill me in the
> womb; so my mother would have been my grave, and
> her womb forever great. Why did I come forth from
> the womb to see toil and sorrow, and spend my days
> in shame? (Jer 20:14–18)

Jeremiah clearly could speak his mind and heart to God,
even in the worst of times. In spite of his reluctance, his
depression, his near despair, he was not a quitter. He never
tempered the word of God to suit his hearers. He seems to
have found enough resources in his relationship with God
to go on to the end. Perhaps his ability to speak so intimately of his weaknesses, his anger, his resentments helped
him to continue to be the prophet God wanted him to be.

Once, after a talk on prayer to a university group, a
social science professor spoke up. He said that he wanted
to pray, desired an intimate relationship with God, but
could not do it because he knew that God would make a
demand of him. He knew what God would ask of him, and
he did not want to do it. As a result he did not pray and did
not have an intimate relationship with God. I responded
spontaneously: "Why don't you tell God you don't want to
do it!" He said: "Can I do that?" I said: "Of course." If I
had the presence of mind, I could have pointed him

toward Jeremiah, the reluctant prophet, who was not afraid to tell God that he did not want to do what God was asking.

The Jesuit poet Gerard Manley Hopkins, no stranger to deep depression and near despair, wrote a poem based on Jeremiah's complaint (Jer 12:1ff):

> Thou art indeed just, Lord, if I contend
> With thee; but, sir, so what I plead is just.
> Why do sinners' ways prosper? and why must
> Disappointment all I endeavor end?
> Wert thou my enemy, O thou my friend,
> How wouldst thou worse, I wonder, than thou dost
> Defeat, thwart me? Oh, the sots and thralls of lust
> Do in spare hours more thrive than I that spend,
> Sir, life upon thy cause. See, banks and brakes
> Now, leavèd how thick! lacèd they are again
> With fretty chervil, look, and fresh wind shakes
> Them; birds build—but not I build; no, but strain,
> Time's eunuch, and not breed one work that wakes.
> Mine, O thou lord of life, send my roots rain.

That Hopkins had some black days and nights we can see from the first verse of "I wake and feel":

> I wake and feel the fell of dark, not day.
> What hours, O what black hours we have spent
> This night! what sights you, heart, saw; ways you went!
> And more must, in yet longer light's delay.

Seemingly, he, too, found some comfort in being able to tell God directly how he was feeling.

John Carmody, whose prayer expressing his love for God we met earlier, was also able to express his anger.

One of the psalms written during his final illness reminds
me of Jeremiah's and Hopkins's complaint:

> You let your people be treated badly.
> Friend after friend has a sad tale to tell.
> The wrong people are in charge,
> venal and unimaginative.
> Has it always been this way?
> I do not understand why.
> What is so hard about telling the truth,
> keeping one's word,
> remembering how pain feels?
> Why do you not smite the wicked,
> teach the obtuse by slashing their flesh?
> In your silence, God, you seem not to care
> and so to sanction the status quo.
> I hate the ways of the wicked,
> and I want you to hate them too.
> Rise up, O God,
> and show yourself our savior.
> If you do not judge
> between sinners and righteous,
> how will we bear the moral life?
> O God of our dying,
> be our just judge.

In another prayer he takes God to task for all the pain in
the world:

> When I go about among your people,
> the pain of so many lays me low.
> Physically or mentally
> pain seems more the rule than the exception.
> Typical faces are lined deep with worry.

I have given up trying to understand.
It makes no sense that the world should run by tor-
ment.
I know nothing else to do
but come before you in protest
asking night and day
that you right this wrong,
supplying the peace that I cannot.
We are not gods.
The best of us can alleviate pain only momentarily.
Why, O God, have you made your people for suffering?
Could you not have arranged things better,
protected your children at their games?
Or is pain some strange show of your kindness for us,
a high way to bring us to heaven?
That does not sound right,
but you can see that I am becoming desperate.
My mind does not know where to turn.
At best, I can only wait and watch and wonder.
One day
you will reveal why things are as they are.
One day
all manner of thing may be well.

Apparently speaking openly and honestly to God
helped John to live and die in some peace. In the last
"generic letter" he and his wife Denise wrote to their family and friends just two months before his death, we read
these words:

It's a roller-coaster life, as perhaps all lives are. The
invitation has been to live fully, gratefully, while
practicing the art of dying...learning to die while loving living. Realizing that an incarnate divinity knows
this biphased rhythm of human existence from

within. Trying therefore to become, not callous about pain or death, nor presumptuous, but free of their power to loom up as frightening idols and block out the far greater reality of God. Any of our lives is a small thing....And yet each of our lives stands before God, comes directly from God, utterly clear in its specificity, for God, having no limits, is not overcome by the swarm of us creatures but in the divine patience out of time can love each of us just for ourselves. So we wait, letting our aging, sickening bodies instruct us as much as our minds, and remembering that we have not been called servants but friends.

In some short stories of Andre Dubus we find a kind of intimacy with God that allows a person to say what is often left unsaid out of fear and shame. See, for example, "A Father's Story" or "Out of Snow." But he has also let us in on his own intimate relationship with God in personal essays published after a terrible accident that left him with only one leg and that one not functioning very well. Some time after the accident his marriage broke up, and he lost custody of his two young daughters, Cadence and Madeleine. In *Broken Vessels* he begins the essay about that loss this way:

> On the twenty-third of June, a Thursday afternoon in 1988, I lay on my bed and looked out the sliding doors at blue sky and green poplars and I wanted to die. I wanted to see You and cry out to You: *So You had three years of public life which probably weren't so bad, were probably even good most of the time, and You suffered for three days, from Gethsemane to Calvary, but You never had children taken away from You.* That is what I wanted to do when I died, but it is not why I wanted to die. I wanted to die because my little girls were in

Montauk on Long Island, and had been there since
Wednesday, and would be till Sunday; and I had last
seen and held and heard them on Tuesday. Cadence
is six, and Madeleine is seventeen months.

Later in the essay he writes about the night terrors that
Cadence was experiencing. They called a pediatrician who
gave them some advice:

I do not remember what she told us to do, because
nothing we did soothed Cadence; she kept crying and
screaming, and I lay helpless on my back, wanting to
rise, and hold her in my arms, and walk with her, and
I yelled at the ceiling, the night sky above it: *You come
down from that cross and give this child some peace!*

Finally he writes:

Today is the twenty-ninth of August 1988, and since
the twenty-third of June, the second of two days when
I wanted to die, I have not wanted my earthly life to
end, have not wanted to confront You with anger and
despair. I receive You in the Eucharist at daily Mass,
and look at You on the cross, but mostly I watch the
priest, and the old deacon, a widower, who brings me
the Eucharist; and the people who walk past me to
receive; and I know they have all endured their own
agony, and prevailed in their own way, though not
alone but drawing their hope and strength from
those they love, those who love them, and from You,
in the sometimes tactile, sometimes incomprehensi-
ble, sometimes seemingly lethal way that You give.
    A week ago I read again *The Old Man and the Sea*,
and learned from it that, above all, our bodies exist to

perform the condition of our spirits: our choices, our desires, our loves. My physical mobility and my little girls have been taken from me; but I remain. So my crippling is a daily and living sculpture of certain truths: we receive and we lose, and we must try to achieve gratitude; and with that gratitude to embrace with whole hearts whatever of life that remains after the losses. No one can do this alone, for being absolutely alone finally means a life not only without people or God or both to love, but without love itself.

He seems to know how to speak the truth to God and seems to have found peace.

We can end this chapter here. We have been discussing how unexpressed anger can put potholes in the road to an intimate relationship with another human being and with God. But in fact, the road to intimacy can be rutted by any cover-up of a significant emotion that has to do with the other. A developing intimate relationship with God may also require that we admit some rather unsavory feelings to God. John Carmody wanted God to hate the ways of the wicked. Jeremiah wanted vengeance on his foes (e.g., Jer 15:15). Some parts of the psalms make us wince (e.g., "Happy shall they be who take your little ones and dash them against the rock!" [Ps 137:9]). Intimacy requires for its continued development a willingness to become totally transparent with the other, even about embarrassing and hurtful things. When we trust God enough to be so transparent, we find that we have lost nothing but our chains and our loneliness.

Chapter 7

Eros, Sexuality and Intimacy with God

W e are gendered and sexual beings. Our gender and our sexuality have a profound influence on all our relationships, including our relationship with God. In chapter 2 we referred to the writer of Psalm 27 as being enamored of God's beauty and indicated that the Hebrew word translated as beauty is related to words referring to "physical charm, erotic and aesthetic enjoyment, the various emotions of friendship, the thrill of learning, and the holy pleasure of liturgical singing" (Terrien). I have reflected on the times when I have felt the "desire for I know not what" of that chapter and realize that there is a sensual, almost erotic element to the desire. It has similarities to the initial erotic attraction I have felt for another human being, an attraction that can lead to falling in love. It is a yearning that affects my whole being. There is a whiff of the erotic in C. S. Lewis's description of the desire for God, and in Frederick Buechner's experience of this desire when, as an adolescent, his knee touched the knee of the young girl on the pier in the Bahamas. Why should this not be the case if we are embodied creatures with senses, feelings and a gendered sexuality? In this chapter I want to explore some aspects of intimacy with God that arise precisely because we are erotic and sexual beings.

Mind you, it is not easy for us to speak honestly and appropriately about the erotic and sexual, even in these more open times. Many of us may remember a time when such matters were not mentioned in "polite society." A personal example may help us to see how we have been trained to avoid references to matters that touch upon, even indirectly, these subjects. As a young Jesuit I had a day home for the first time since I had entered the Society of Jesus. Some friends of my sisters happened to pay a visit. After they left, I asked, quite matter-of-factly, "Is Joan pregnant?" My sister piped up: "Bill, we don't use that word in this house." Clearly my family did not encourage talk about matters of eros and sexuality. Others may be able to remember similar experiences. It is no wonder that people of my generation have a hard time talking about eros and sexuality, even with the God who made us sexual beings.

After my mother died, it dawned on me that she now knew things about my affective and sexual life that I would never have told her while she was alive. There is nothing that I need to be ashamed to let her know, unless I am ashamed to let myself and God know it. This realization helped me to recognize that I had not been communicating with God about my erotic and sexual longings except to beg pardon for what I considered sins. Even though I could say that God had made me a sexual person, it seemed ingrained in me that we did not talk about such things with anyone else, even God, except to confess transgressions against the sixth and ninth commandments. Entering the Society of Jesus was not much help, at least in my early years. In the *Constitutions of the Society of Jesus* Ignatius of Loyola writes: "What pertains to the vow of chastity requires no interpretation, since it is evident how perfectly it should be preserved, by endeavoring to imitate therein the purity of the angels in cleanness of body and mind. Therefore, with this presupposed, we shall now treat of holy obedience." Clearly this point of view did not invite open discussion of sexuality either with the Lord, with a spiritual director or with anyone else for that matter. Though in the course of growing up as a Jesuit I became free of some of my inhibitions, I still did not talk about my erotic and sexual desires with God. In this area of my life, in other words, I was in hiding almost as much as I had been with my mother when she was alive. As a result, I believe, my relationship with God was not as intimate as it could have been. It was not easy, and is still not easy, to speak openly about these matters with God. But I have gotten better at it, and I have gotten better at sharing such matters in prayer with my mother as well.

I mention this personal vignette at the beginning of this chapter because it ties in with the thoughts of the previous chapter. Just as our relationship with God can lose vitality when we are unwilling to communicate our feelings of anger, resentment and hatred, so too it can lose vitality if we are unwilling to speak of our erotic and sexual feelings, desires and activities when they take center stage in our lives. And for most of us they often do take center stage. Perhaps one reason why our prayer life languishes is our fear of speaking honestly about these matters with God. I have to say that my own prayer has recovered life when my erotic and sexual impulses, feelings and drives have pushed to the fore and I have been able to talk honestly with God about them.

Whether we are single or married, heterosexual or homosexual, lay person, priest or member of a religious congregation, we are called as Christians to try to live chaste lives. To do so is a struggle, as we know. In his sonnet "Batter My Heart, Three-Personed God" John Donne expressed something that rings true. Many of us believe that chastity is within our power to attain. Donne, it seems, came to a different conclusion, and from the sound of the sonnet he came to his conclusion from bitter experience:

> Batter my heart, three-personed God; for You
> As yet but knock, breathe, shine, and seek to mend;
> That I may rise and stand, o'erthrow me, and bend
> Your force to break, blow, burn, and make me new.
> I, like an usurped town, to another due,
> Labor to admit You, but O, to no end;
> Reason, Your viceroy in me, me should defend,
> But is captived, and proves weak or untrue.
> Yet dearly I love You, and would be lovèd fain,
> But am betrothed unto Your enemy.
> Divorce me, untie or break that knot again;
> Take me to You, imprison me, for I,
> Except you enthrall me, never shall be free,
> Nor ever chaste, except You ravish me.

Donne admits that he cannot control his sexual desires, cannot be chaste, unless God draws him, attracts him, gives him both the grace and the motivation to be chaste. Without denying or denigrating the usefulness of traditional ascetic practices, we might take a lesson from John Donne and speak honestly to the Lord about our joys, our struggles, our fantasies, our desires, asking that God become so attractive that we can live chastely with freedom and joy. If we do not speak openly and ask God's help, but rather try by our own efforts to control our passions and desires, we will become self-absorbed, perhaps crabbed and unloving, and guilt-ridden. A test of whether we are on intimate terms with the Lord might well be whether we can speak honestly about these passions and desires and ask God's help to live as we believe we are called to live.

In his major work on Christianity and sexuality, *Body and Society,* Peter Brown notes that the monks of the desert had to come to terms with the permanence of sexual fantasy:

> Because of this observed quality of permanence, sexual desire was now treated as effectively coextensive with human nature. Abiding awareness of the self as a sexual being, forever subject to sexual longings, and troubled—even in dreams—by sexual fantasies highlighted the areas of intractability in the human person. But this intractability was not simply physical. It pointed into the very depths of the soul. Sexual desire revealed the knot of unsurrendered privacy that lay at the very heart of fallen man. Thus, in the new language of the desert, sexuality became, as it were, an ideogram of the unopened heart. As a result, the abatement of sexual fantasy in the heart of the monk—an abatement that was held to be accompanied, quite concretely, with a cessation of the monk's night emissions—signaled, in the body, the ascetic's final victory over the closed heart. Only the hand of Christ Himself, reaching down from heaven...could snatch the monk out of the tomb of his private will, by overcoming in him that most ineradicably private of his drives. To receive from Christ the grace of a transparent chastity was to shatter the last weapons of the unsurrendered will: it was to complete the transformation of the heart.

For the desert monk, therefore, the issue of chastity was not an issue of the body so much as of the heart. The monk was being asked to become transparent before God, as we all are, and that meant being willing to open the most private areas of one's heart to God, and to a spiritual director. For the monks of the desert, and perhaps for all of us, one of the most private areas has to do with our sexual desires and fantasies. Brown also makes clear that these ascetics did not consider sexual temptations the most dangerous. The spiritual dangers that often overshadowed them were "the dull aches of pride and resentment and...dread onslaughts of immoderate spiritual ambition. These could rock whole monasteries, destroying lives and littering the literature of the desert with chilling accounts of pathological cases of hatred, hallucinations, and dire ego-inflation." The monks were asked to become transparent before God, and sexuality was, for them as well as for many who have come after them, the most difficult to open to the light of God.

The quotation of Donne's sonnet allows a convenient segue to the issue of erotic and sexual attraction to the divine. Donne tells God that he can never be chaste unless God ravish him. The word *ravish* is given a number of meanings in dictionaries: "to seize and carry away by violence"; "to remove from one place or state to another (as from earth to heaven)"; "to transport with emotion and especially with joy or delight." In the first meaning it also carries, often enough, the sense of rape. At the least Donne asks that God transport him with emotion and delight, but also to transport him from a place of unchastity to that of chastity. Could he also be asking God to become erotically and even sexually attractive? We are reminded of Jeremiah's strong, near blasphemous complaint to God: "O Lord, you have enticed me, and I was enticed; you have overpowered me, and you have prevailed" (Jer 20:7). In his *Anchor Bible* volume on Jeremiah John Bright translates the first part of this verse: "You have seduced me, Yahweh, and I let you." Again the word used can have multiple meanings, because the same word is used in verse 20, where Jeremiah says that his enemies are whispering: "Perhaps he can be enticed, and we can prevail against

him, and take our revenge on him" (Jer 20:20). Here
Bright translates the word as "tricked." Nonetheless, in
both English and Hebrew, the words used by Donne and by
Jeremiah have a sexual connotation. Are we, or at least
some of us, sexually attracted to God?

I have already alluded to the erotic overtones of the
desire for "I know not what." Given the fact that our sexuality pervades our being, it would be strange indeed if the
attraction to God had no erotic or sexual overtones. Some
of the psalms speak of the longing for God in language
redolent of the erotic, as we have noted. Some mystics
speak and write in similar language. These words from
Teresa of Avila's autobiography indicate that her love for
God eventually became strong enough to overcome her
love for her father, a love that must have been tinged with
the erotic. She describes the difficulty of leaving her father
and family when she entered the convent:

> I remember, clearly and truly, that when I left my
> father's house I felt that separation so keenly that the
> feeling will not be greater, I think, when I die. For it
> seemed that every bone in my body was being sun-
> dered. Since there was no love of God to take away my
> love for my father and relatives, everything so con-
> strained me that if the Lord hadn't helped me, my
> reflections would not have been enough for me to
> continue on. In this situation He gave me such
> courage against myself that I carried out the task.

Obviously Teresa came to love God passionately. For
example, in her "Spiritual Testimonies" she writes:

> At other times I receive a very intense, consuming
> impulse for God that I cannot resist. It seems my life

is coming to an end, and so this impulse makes me cry out and call to God; and it comes with great frenzy. Sometimes I'm unable to remain seated because of the vomitings from which I suffer; and this pain comes upon me without my seeking it. It is of such a kind that the soul would never want to be relieved of it as long as it lives. I have longings not to live this apparent life any more. I cannot find any remedy for these longings, since the cure for the desire to see God is death; and I cannot take this cure. Along with this, it seems to my soul that everyone has the greatest consolation except itself and that all find a cure for their trials except itself. This causes such affliction that if the Lord didn't provide a remedy by means of a certain rapture, in which everything is made peaceful and the soul remains in deep quiet and satisfaction—now beholding something of what it desires, now understanding other things—it would be impossible to get free from that pain.

The strength of this passion for God can be sensed in these words from the same source:

When I see something beautiful or rich, like water, fields, flowers, fragrances, music, and so on, it seems to me that I wouldn't want to see or hear these things, so great is the difference between them and what I am accustomed to seeing; thus all desire for such things is taken from me. And as a result I have come to care so little for them that, save for the first stirrings, they make no impression on me and seem like dung.

In the same spiritual testimonies Teresa speaks of being made a bride of her Lord, of receiving a beautiful ring signifying this espousal. It is hardly surprising, therefore, that the Song of Songs should have had a strong impact on her interior life, even though she seems to have been able to read very little of that book in Spanish. It would be helpful, now, to examine that book of the Bible.

Moses Maimonides, the famous Jewish philosopher of the Middle Ages, writes that anyone who loves God "is like a lovesick man whose mind is never free from his love for a certain woman and grows in it whether sitting or rising, both when eating and drinking—greater even than this must be the love of God in the heart of his lovers who continually grow more fervent" (cited in Vacek). Maimonides then cites the Song of Songs as an allegory on this theme. Both Jewish and Christian writers have argued that this book speaks of the love between God and God's chosen people, and between God and the individual. Yet the book seems to be a collection of love poems that speak in starkly erotic, sensual and sexual imagery of the love between a man and a woman. One of the key questions down the ages has been: "Why is this book in the canon of sacred writings?" The answers have run the gamut from statements such as Maimonides' that the book is only an allegory of the love between God and the human soul to statements that the book is a glorification of the love that God wants to prevail between husband and wife. Many modern biblical scholars would argue that the book is not an allegory, but speaks of human, physical love. In his *Anchor Bible* commentary, Marvin Pope remarks:

> Nevertheless, the instincts and insights that from the beginning led both Christian and Jewish exegetes to relate the language of the Song to divine and superhuman love were based on internal evidence largely ignored by recent interpreters....Sexuality is a basic

human interest and the affirmation that "God is Love" includes all meanings of both words.

Pope thinks it possible that the poems use the image of a woman longing for her absent lover, who has gone away on a caravan to make his wealth, to express the longing of Israel as a people and of individual Israelites for God. The author of the Song "saw the erotic longing of the maiden as a simile for the need of man for God." The poems, however, express not only the longing of the woman for her lover, but also the sensual and erotic delight and desire of the man for the woman. As Marcia Falk has pointed out, these love songs indicate a reciprocity between the man and the woman that breaks with stereotypes of the active man and the passive woman. Both male and female speakers actively beckon their beloved. If the Song, then, is about the relation of God and Israel, then the author of the Song writes not only from the point view of Israel or of the individual Israelite longing for God, but also from the point of view of God, a God who passionately longs for his people.

Teresa of Avila wrote some meditations on the Song of Songs. She was thrilled to hear the words "Let the Lord kiss me with the kiss of his mouth, for Your breasts are better than wine," because they seemed to give her permission to express what she was feeling. She writes of herself:

> I know someone who for a number of years had many fears, and nothing gave her assurance, but the Lord was pleased that she hear some words from the Song of Songs, and through them she understood that her soul was being well guided. As I have said, she understood that it was possible for a soul in love with its Spouse to experience all these favors, swoons, deaths, afflictions, delights, and joys in relation to Him.

When she heard the sensual and erotic words of the Song of Songs, she was relieved because they echoed her own strong passion for her God, her Lover, her Spouse. The ecstasy of Teresa's passionate love for God and of God for her is depicted in the sculpture of Giovanni Bernini in the church of S. Maria della Vittoria in Rome where she receives the divine arrow of love.

Her disciple and coworker in the reform of Carmel in Spain, John of the Cross, speaks in similar language in his own poems, which are considered masterpieces of the Spanish language. Here are a few examples from the volume compiled by Willis Barnstone:

From "Dark Night":

On a dark secret night,
starving for love and deep in flame,
O happy lucky flight!
unseen I slipped away,
my house at last was calm and safe.

....

O night, my guide!
O night more friendly than the dawn!
O tender night that tied
lover and the loved one,
loved one in the lover fused as one!
On my flowering breasts
which I had saved for him alone,
he slept and I caressed
and fondled him with love,
and cedars fanned the air above.

From "Spiritual Canticle":

BRIDE

Deep in the winevault of
my love I drank, and when I came
　　out on this open meadow
　　I knew no thing at all,
I lost the flock I used to drive.
　　He held me to his chest
and taught me a sweet science.
　　Instantly I yielded all
　　I had—keeping nothing—
and promised then to be his bride.
　　I gave my soul to him
and all the things I owned were his:
　　I have no flock to tend
　　nor any other trade
and my one ministry is love....

BRIDEGROOM

My bride has gone into
the pleasant garden she desired,
　　and lies upon the grass
　　happy, resting her neck
in the gentle arms of her love.
　　Under the apple tree
you came and were engaged to me;
　　there I gave you my hand
　　and you were then redeemed
where once your mother had been raped....

BRIDE

Let us be happy, darling,
and see us mirrored in your beauty
    on mountains and the hills
    where limpid waters plash;
let us go deeper in the wood.
And then we'll climb high, high
to peaks riddled with stony caves
    safely hidden away,
    and there we'll go inside
and taste the pomegranate wine....

Obviously this great mystical poet could express what had happened to him in his union with God only through the language of erotic human love.

Some might wonder about the psychological health of such expressive passion. Yet both Teresa and John were anything but self-centered neurotics, as can be seen from their lives. Of course, they were human beings, and, as such, as neurotic as any of us. But these levels of intimacy with God seemed to have made them capable of loving others, of working hard and of bearing pain and even persecution without a hint of bitterness or resentment. If we take the injunction of Jesus to heart, "You will know them by their fruits" (Mt 7:16), then we can say that the passionate love that Teresa and John had for God, and their own acknowledgment of God's passionate love for them, were clearly desired by God. It also needs to be said that the path to such passionate intimacy with God led through much darkness and a great deal of mortification of their self-love. Perhaps in these mystics of God's passionate love we have paradigms of what is possible for those who are willing to be totally transparent before God.

Their whole being, including their bodies, were caught up in relationship of intimacy with God.

In his highly acclaimed novel, *Mariette in Ecstasy*, Ron Hansen depicts a teenager who, like Thérèse of Lisieux, enters a cloistered convent where her older sister is prioress. Mariette is seventeen years old as the novel opens in 1906 with the preparations for her entrance into the convent in upstate New York. Mariette is sitting in her nightgown penning instructions about the distribution of her things.

> She then stands and unties the strings at her neck so that the pink satin seeps onto a green Chinese carpet that is as plush as grass. And she is held inside an upright floor mirror, pretty and naked and seventeen. She skeins her chocolate-brown hair. She pouts her mouth. She esteems her full breasts as she has seen men esteem them. She haunts her milk-white skin with her hands.

> *Even this I give You.*

The novel depicts a real young woman with all the tangled motivations of any teenager who enters a contemplative convent. But it also seems clear that her deepest motivation is the love of God. She writes to the priest confessor of her love for Jesus, of her desire to give herself entirely to him and of his promise to her that she would have much to suffer. She has great consolation, but also great desolation when she cannot find any comfort in prayer. In the convent itself she becomes a bone of contention, some looking upon her as a budding saint, others as a charlatan. At one point her sister, the prioress, who is dying of cancer, says to her: "'You're my sister, but I don't understand you. You aren't understandable.' She smiles. 'You may be a saint. Saints are like that, I think. Elusive. Other.

Upsetting.'" Then after her sister's death Mariette receives the stigmata, which further polarizes the convent and brings unwanted publicity in the neighborhood. She describes to Father Marriot her experience:

> I felt greatly upset at first because of Annie, Mother Céline [her sister]; but as I began to meditate on the crucifixion and Christ's own trials in this world, I became rapt in thought and I found myself again before Jesus, who was suffering such terrible pain. He was horrible with blood and his breathing was hard and troubled, but his pain had less to do with that than with his human sense of failure, injustice, and loneliness. An unquenchable desire to join him in his agonies took hold of me then, as if I could halve his afflictions by sharing them, and I beseeched Jesus to grant me that grace. And, in his great kindness, he gratified me at once. Kneeling there below his cross, I saw that blood no longer issued from his wounds, but only flashing light as hot as fire. And all of a sudden I felt a keen hurt as those flames touched my hands and feet and heart. I have never felt such pain before, and I have never been so happy. I have no memories of the hours passing, I have only the memories of a kind of pleasure and contentment I haven't ever known, a kind that made me love the world as he does, and hearing him whisper just before dawn that I ought to go to you.

Father Marriot, using the test of the "fruits," discerns that Mariette is a genuine mystic in love with Jesus. Because of the disruption she brings into the convent, Mariette is sent home, where she tends her father until his death. At the end of the novel, thirty years later, she writes to one of her fellow novices who has become prioress. She talks of her ordinary life of work and prayer, and then ends with these words, which also end the novel:

> And yet sometimes I am so sad. Even when I have friends over often for tea or canasta, there is a Great Silence here for weeks and weeks, and the Devil tells me the years since age seventeen have been a great abeyance and I have been like a troubled bride pining each night for a husband who is lost without a trace.
>
> Children stare in the grocery as if they know ghostly stories about me, and I hear the hushed talk when I hobble by or lose the hold in my hands, but Christ reminds me, as he did in my greatest distress, that he loves me more, now that I am despised, than when I was so richly admired in the past.
>
> And Christ still sends me roses. We try to be formed and held and kept by him, but instead he offers us freedom. And now when I try to know his will, his kindness floods me, his great love overwhelms me, and I hear him whisper, Surprise me.

Obviously Hansen, the novelist, has done a great deal of research on mystics, on stigmata, and on the discernment of spirits. I believe he tells the story of a real woman who is in love with Jesus.

As we come to the end of this discussion of eros, sexuality and intimacy with God, I want to look at a possible explanation for the use of erotic and sexual imagery to describe the love relationship between God and God's people. Sebastian Moore suggests that we may have things the wrong way round when we use the analogy of the love relationship between two human beings to illuminate the love relationship between God and us.

The supposition is that the bedrock reality, that which
the prophet fundamentally has in mind, is the mutual
love of man and woman, *to* which he is comparing the
less known relationship between the human spirit and
God. Once you have a taste of the luminous self and its
longing, you see that it's the other way round. The
bedrock reality for the prophet, the fundamental thing
he/she has in mind, is the grounding sense of the self-
in-God, *from* which he is deriving the significance of
the love between man and woman.

In other words, the author of the Song of Songs had the
experience of a passionate relationship between him-
self/herself and God and used this experience to illuminate the love between two human beings. So too, Teresa of
Avila and John of the Cross, who, as far as we know, did
not know the intimacies of a love relationship between a
man and a woman, are describing their love relationship
with God in language that illuminates what might charac-
terize all love relationships that are in right order.

One day when I was pondering in prayer these questions, I asked this question of God: "Is it dangerous for you
to let yourself be seen as engaged in such a reciprocal relationship with human beings?" What I felt I heard was
something like this: "With all you know of me do you think
that I would worry about such things? I want to draw you
human beings into an intimate relationship. When you
are allured, when you realize that your deepest happiness
lies in being one with me, then you can gradually be
taught that the delights of the relationship are not what
you want, but me; then you will learn through what is
called the dark night that I am God and not you. But first
you have to recognize your desire for me and let it be the
engine of your life." Reciprocity in the relationship is
desired by God, but God cannot be other than God.

Finally, is God a jealous God who cannot bear other loves in our lives? Sometimes we can get that impression when we read the lives of saints such as Teresa of Avila. But she was a very loving woman, a woman who had friends of both sexes. My friend John Carmody loved God fiercely, as we read in an earlier chapter and as his widow told me. But he also loved Denise passionately, and he loved his friends deeply, warmly and honestly. What all of us who succumb to the deepest desire of our hearts, namely, the desire for God, come to realize is that the more we love God, the more we are enabled to love others. Peter Brown writes of Anthony of the Desert:

> The greatest sign of Anthony's recovery of the state of Adam was not his taut body. In his very last years, this state was revealed ever more frequently in the quintessentially fourth-century gift of sociability. He came to radiate such magnetic charm, and openness to all, that any stranger who came upon him, surrounded by crowds of disciples, visiting monks and lay pilgrims, would know at once, in that dense press of black-garbed figures, which one was the great Anthony. He was instantly recognizable as someone whose heart had achieved total transparency to others.

And Mariette said to Father Marriot: "I have no memories of the hours passing, I have only the memories of a kind of pleasure and contentment I haven't ever known, a kind that made me love the world as he does." God is a jealous lover in the sense that there is only one God who will ultimately still our hunger, but God wants us to love all our brothers and sisters and the whole of creation as ourselves.

Chapter 8

Darkness, Pain and Intimacy with God

In the course of the last chapter we heard not only of passionate desire for God, but also of great pain and darkness. Teresa of Avila wrote of the great pain she experienced, but a pain that she would not want to relinquish. She also suffered from misunderstandings of her call to reform Carmel, but she remained calm and peaceful throughout. Teresa and a companion had come to the conclusion that they were being called to begin a new foundation of Carmelites and had obtained the permission of the provincial, who then changed his mind. Teresa writes:

> I was very much disliked throughout my monastery because I wanted to found a more enclosed monastery. They said I was insulting them; that in my own monastery I could also serve God since there were others in it better than I; that I had no love for the house; that it would be better to procure income for this place than for some other. Several of them said I should be thrown into the prison cell....Yet since I couldn't mention the main factor, which was that the

Lord had commanded me to do this, I didn't know how to act; so I remained silent about the other things. God granted me the very great favor that none of all this disturbed me; rather, I gave up the plan with as much ease and contentment as I would have if it hadn't cost me anything. No one could believe this, not even the very persons of prayer who knew me. They thought that I was very afflicted and ashamed....As for myself, since it seemed to me I had done everything I could, I thought I wasn't obliged to do what the Lord had commanded me; and I remained in the house, for I was very satisfied and pleased there. Although I could never stop believing that the foundation would come about, I no longer saw the means, nor did I know how or when; but I was very certain that it would.

Her sufferings were nothing compared to those of John of the Cross, who was actually imprisoned by his brother Carmelites who fought the reform of Carmel John had begun under Teresa's tutelage. He was thrown into a narrow cell and was brought each day to the refectory where he was given bread, water and sardine scraps on the floor. Then he was beaten on his bare back by the leather whips of the monks. In his cell he was infested with lice since he was given no change of clothes for six months. Yet during this time of imprisonment he began writing his "Spiritual Canticle," "The Fountain" and "Dark Night," some of the greatest poems in the Spanish language, poems expressing his great love for and joy in God.

I am reminded of the scene in the Acts of the Apostles where the apostles are flogged by order of the chief priests and ordered not to speak in the name of Jesus. "As they left the council, they rejoiced that they were considered worthy to suffer dishonor for the sake of the name. And every day in the temple and at home they did not cease to teach and proclaim Jesus as the Messiah" (Acts 5:41–42).

Those who get close to God or to God's son, Jesus, seem to draw fire even from those who should be on God's side. We have already seen how Jeremiah was treated by the leaders of God's people when he told the truth that he heard from God. Jesus himself was crucified, and he promised his disciples that they would suffer for his name's sake. Just as intimacy with God is resisted by each one of us in one way or another, so too, perhaps, we are tempted to mistrust and suspect those who have let God come close; they may make us uncomfortable not only because they remind us of what we are resisting but also perhaps because they bring God too close for comfort. It is something to ponder.

What is striking in the cases of Teresa of Avila and John of the Cross is that they maintained such joy, peace and charity throughout their trials. Although Jeremiah seems to be an argument to the contrary, we still have abundant witnesses to the fact that closeness to God helps people to bear great suffering. Recently I was moved to read that the martyrs of Nagasaki who were crucified in 1597 burst into song when they saw the crosses waiting for them and then rushed to wait for the executioners to fasten them. On that occasion Paul Miki, a Jesuit seminarian, preached his final sermon: he invited the onlookers to accept Christianity, said that he was joyfully giving his life for Christ, and then forgave his executioners. There is something profoundly mysterious in the way those who love God with a passion suffer and at the same time exude joy.

Nor does one have to be Christian. Etty Hillesum, the young Dutch Jewess who died in Auschwitz, left an amazing diary of her last couple of years of life, a diary of the gradual development of a deep love of God even as she saw the evil darkness of Nazism engulfing her and her people. A short time before being shipped to Auschwitz and her death she wrote this "Sunday morning prayer" in her diary:

> Dear God, these are anxious times. Tonight for the first time I lay in the dark with burning eyes as scene after scene of human suffering passed before me. I shall promise You one thing, God, just one thing: I shall never burden my today with cares about my tomorrow, although that takes some practice. Each day is sufficient unto itself. I shall try to help You, God, to stop my strength ebbing away, though I cannot vouch for it in advance. But one thing is becoming increasingly clear to me: that You cannot help us, that we must help You to help ourselves. And that is all we can manage these days and also all that really matters: that we safeguard that little piece of You, God, in ourselves. And perhaps in others as well. Alas, there doesn't seem much You Yourself can do about our circumstances, about our lives. Neither do I hold You responsible. You cannot help us but we must help You and defend Your dwelling place inside us to the last....And there are those who want to put their bodies in safe keeping....And they say, "I shan't let them get me into their clutches." But they forget that no one is in their clutches who is in Your arms. I am beginning to feel a little more peaceful, God, thanks to this conversation with You.

It is mysterious, indeed, what closeness to God can do for someone in pain. But it also may make sense. When we allow God to come close, we realize that all else, even suffering and death, is ultimately dung, as Teresa of Avila wrote. Those who have come close to God know, it seems, the truth of St. Paul's statement:

Yet whatever gains I had, these I have come to regard
as loss because of Christ. More than that, I regard
everything as loss because of the surpassing value of
knowing Christ Jesus my Lord. For his sake I have suffered the loss of all things, and I regard them as rub-
bish, in order that I may gain Christ and be found in
him, not having a righteousness of my own that
comes from the law, but one that comes through faith
in Christ, the righteousness from God based on faith.
I want to know Christ and the power of his resurrection and the sharing of his sufferings by becoming
like him in his death, if somehow I may attain the resurrection from the dead. (Phil 3:7–11)

Some of the pain experienced by those who come close
to God seems to come from God. Near the end of the last
chapter I mentioned that God seems to use the dark night
of the senses and of the soul to draw a person away from a
love of consolation to a real love of God. In *Mariette in
Ecstasy* Mariette writes to her confessor:

At this time I am only permitted to tell you that Our
Lord has promised that I will suffer great pain in the
course of my life. Christ has told me that soon he will
put my faith to the proof and find out whether I truly
love him and whether the offering of my heart which
I so often have made to him is authentic.

Christ said, "You will grow hard, Mariette. You will
find yourself afflicted and empty and tempted, and
all your body's senses will then revolt and become
like wolves. Each of the world's tawdry pleasures will
invade your sleep. Your memories will be sad and persistent. Everything that is contrary to God will be in
your sight and thinking, and all that is of and from
God you'll no longer feel. I shall not offer comfort at

such times, but I shall not cease to understand you. I shall allow Satan to harshly attack your soul, and he will plant a great hatred of prayer in your heart, and a hundred evil thoughts in your mind, and terror of him will never leave you.

"You will have no solace or pity, not even from your superiors. You will be tortured by gross outrages and mistreatment, but no one will believe you. You will be punished and humbled and greatly confused, and heaven will seem closed to you. God will seem dead and indifferent, you will try to be recollected, but instead be distracted, you will try to pray and your thoughts will fly, you will seek me fruitlessly and without avail for I shall hide in noise and shadows and I shall seem to withdraw when you need me most. Everyone will seem to abandon you. Confession will seem tedious, Communion stale and unprofitable; you will practice each daily exercise of worship and devotion, but all through necessity, as if you stood outside yourself and hated what you'd become. And yet you will believe, Mariette, but as if you did not believe; you will always hope, but as if you did not hope; you will love your Savior, but as if you did not love him, because in this time your true feelings will fail you, you will be tired of life and afraid of death, and you will not even have the relief of being able to weep."

This is the novelist's re-creation of what many mystics describe as the "dark night of the soul." In the course of the novel, as we have seen, Mariette does experience what God has promised. But rather amazingly she continues to grow in her love of her Lord and in kindness and openness to others.

Those who experience dryness in prayer will find much help in Thomas Green's *When the Well Runs Dry*. Green wrote the book for readers of his first book on prayer who asked him for help with the times of dryness and darkness that seemed to be their lot once the initial fervor of intimacy with the Lord was over. He draws on the masters of the spiritual life and on his own experience both as a praying person himself and as a spiritual director. I want to underline the importance he places on continuing to pray even when the road is dark and difficult. *"Il faut des rites,"* "Rites are necessary," as the fox tells St. Exupéry's Little Prince. In addition, during periods of darkness or desolation we do well to remember the advice of Ignatius of Loyola, namely, to recall the consolation of the past and to remember the consolation that will surely come. A remark by the divorced Luke Ripley in Andre Dubus's "A Father's Story" seems apropos of both these pieces of advice. He is reflecting on his failed marriage:

> It is not hard to live through a day, if you can live through a moment. What creates despair is the imagination, which pretends that there is a future, and insists on predicting millions of moments, thousands of days, and so drains you that you cannot live the moment at hand. That is what Father Paul told me in those first two years, on some of the bad nights when I believed I could not bear what I had to: the most painful loss was my children, then the loss of Gloria, whom I still loved despite or maybe because of our long periods of sadness that rendered us helpless, so neither of us could break out of it to give a hand to the other. Twelve years later I believe ritual would have healed us more quickly than the repetitious talks we had, perhaps even kept us healed. Marriages have lost that, and I wish I had known then what I know now, and we had performed certain acts together every day, no matter how we felt, and perhaps then we

could have subordinated feeling to action, for surely that is the essence of love. I know this from my distractions during Mass, and during everything else I do, so that my actions and feelings are seldom one. It does not happen every day, but in proportion to everything else in a day, it is rare, like joy.

Thus, in the first place, when in darkness, we need to remember that it is a temptation to begin to project years of darkness; we just need to get through this day. Second, we need to continue our regular prayer, the ritual that undergirds our relationship with God. Those who continue to pray in spite of the darkness and dryness attest to the fact that, like Mariette, God does send them roses.

Of course, one of the pains of the passionate longing for God is that we cannot have what we want, complete union with God. Only the three Persons in the one God are so unique that they are also absolutely one. Perhaps the pain of not being perfectly one with God comes from the fact that we are made in the image of God who is One-in-Three. In other words, the prime analogue for love is God; we are pale images of the Trinity. The three Persons of the Trinity are so united that they are one God. The image for the Trinity used by the Greek Fathers is one of a dance. They use the term *perichoeresis,* where *peri* means "around" and *choeresis* means "dancing." In fact, our word *choir* derives from this last word. As I pondered this image, I thought of African American gospel choirs, who not only sing but also dance and sway and clap their hands. Like whirling dervishes the Trinity dance and clap and sing around one another so fast that they are completely one. We are pale images of such unity. We are made for intimate relationships and especially for union with God, but we cannot be as completely one with God and with those we love as the three Persons who are the one God. Perhaps the pain we experience at not being able to be totally one with those we love comes because we are images of God, but cannot be God. Perhaps the beatitude of life after death will derive from the fact we will be able to dance around as fast as we can and will completely accept with gratitude and joy that we are not God, an acceptance that is very difficult for us.

III.

Intimacy with Jesus

Chapter 9

Jesus, A Man of His Times

When a person makes the full Spiritual Exercises of Ignatius of Loyola, the awakening of the desire to know Jesus better marks a turning point in her journey to intimacy with the Lord. Before this time she has wanted to know of God's love for her, to know that God still loves her in spite of her failures as a human being and a Christian and in spite of her sinful tendencies. She has wanted to be freed from those addictive and self-defeating urges that keep her unhappy and estranged from God and other people. If she has contemplated Jesus in the gospels, she has done so with the desire that he would heal her, would cure her of her blindness and would forgive her sins. The focus has been on her need for love and help. When she can look into the eyes of Jesus dying on the cross and there find love and forgiveness, she finds herself profoundly free and may then spontaneously desire to know Jesus better in order to love him more deeply and follow him more closely. The focus has shifted from a desire to experience God's and Jesus' forgiveness to a desire to have Jesus reveal himself, his loves, his desires, his hopes, his fears, his hates, and so forth. She wants to develop a relationship of mutual intimacy with Jesus.

In 1963, I made the full Spiritual Exercises for the second time as a Jesuit. I had been ordained a priest the year before and now was in the last period of formation before final vows. During that retreat, for the first time in my thirteen years as a Jesuit, a "companion of Jesus," I told him that I loved him. It was a turning point in my life, and the memory of that moment or moments carried me through the following years of graduate studies and the turmoil of the post-Vatican II church. But the relationship did not remain stagnant. Since that time I have continued to learn more about Jesus, not only through contemplative prayer but also through reading. The Jesus I now know intimately has changed considerably. For one thing he has become much more human and believable as human. He is much less a prisoner of my scholastic philosophy and theology training, which tended to remove him from the ordinary human experience I know and knew. In the next three chapters I want to explore intimacy with Jesus, the Jewish man who grew up in Nazareth of Galilee. I believe that knowing this Jesus intimately will be as great a help to others as it has been for me.

Ignatius, as many know, asks the retreatant who desires to know Jesus better to contemplate the gospels. He proposes that retreatants enter the imaginative world of the gospel text with the hope that Jesus will reveal himself to them. He gives models of the method he proposes in the contemplations on the incarnation and nativity. For example, the first point of the contemplation on the incarnation:

> I will see the various persons, some here, some there.
> First, those on the face of the earth, so diverse in dress and behavior: some white and others black, some in peace and others at war, some weeping and

others laughing, some healthy and others sick, some being born and others dying, and so forth.

Second, I will see and consider the three Divine Persons, seated, so to speak, on the royal canopied throne of Their Divine Majesty. They are gazing on the whole face and circuit of the earth; and they see all the peoples in such great blindness, and how they are dying and going down to hell.

Third, I will see Our Lady and the angel greeting her. Then I will reflect on this to draw some profit from what I see.

In the second and third points he suggests that the retreatant listen to what the persons are saying and consider what they are doing. Clearly, Ignatius expects that the retreatant will enter imaginatively into the scene limned in the gospel text. Clearly, too, Ignatius expects that the retreatant's imagination will embellish the text. In this he is following a tradition in the church that has read the gospels (and indeed, much of the Bible) as imaginative literature written to help the people of God to know God and God's ways. Many of the books of the Bible tell stories, imaginative literature describing historical events, whose purpose is not to teach abstract truths about God, but to reveal who God is and how God wants to relate to the people and wants them to relate to God and to one another. They are meant to rouse the imagination, to inflame the heart, to inspire action as much as to instruct the mind. Ignatius seems to trust that God will use the person's imagination as a vehicle to respond to the personal desire to know Jesus better in order to love him more deeply.

Ignatius, like every other human being, was a man of his time, and he used the scriptures as a man of his time. It would not have occurred to him, I believe, to wonder whether the events described in the Bible happened as they are depicted. Thus, he would never have entertained the modern question about how much we can know about the historical Jesus of Nazareth. For all that, like many before him and since, he did come to know Jesus better through his imaginative use of the gospels. So too, people of our time can come to know Jesus better without much knowledge of modern scriptural research. In 1963 I knew something about such research, but it did not enter into my contemplation of the gospels very much. Nevertheless, I believe, I did get to know Jesus more intimately. Scripture scholarship has not stood still in the interim and has had a great public impact, especially on educated Catholics. Many of the readers of this book will be aware that modern scriptural research has raised questions about the "historicity" of the gospels. If nothing else, the popularizing of the so-called findings of the Jesus Seminar in the United States through cover articles in such magazines as *Time* and *Newsweek* has made many people curious, if not doubtful, about what we can actually know about the historical Jesus. So, when we approach the scriptures with the desire to know Jesus better, we may wonder what Jesus we can expect to meet.

A recent experience brought home to me how easily loose talk about the historical Jesus can upset people. A woman who has been a spiritual director for many years began her annual retreat deeply disturbed. She had been in a conversation with a friend whom she admired, another believing woman of a scholarly bent, informed and articulate. This woman had participated in a discussion of the resurrection of the dead at a divinity school. What the resurrection really means, she said, is that the dead live on in the memory of their loved ones. The woman on retreat was very disturbed by this conversation. Everything to which she had given her life seemed to be threatened. If this were true of those she loved, such as her parents, what about the resurrection of Jesus? Did he really rise from the dead, or did he only live on in the memory of his closest followers? Her agony, when she began to talk about the discussion, was intense.

Christianity, like Judaism, is a historical religion. Christians believe that Jesus of Nazareth in Galilee, a Jew of the first century of our era, was crucified by the Romans, died and was buried and, against all expectations, was raised from the dead and was seen by his closest followers. Some modern scripture scholars have concluded that we cannot know the Jesus of history, that we can only know the Christ of our faith. In effect, they are saying that the historical Jesus is irrelevant to our faith; what matters is our existential commitment to the Christ of our faith. The retreatant's friend, I believe, was speaking, at least in part, from this perspective when she said that the resurrection means only that those who die, including Jesus, live on in our memory. I am reminded of a letter by the novelist Flannery O'Connor in which she describes a dinner party at writer Mary McCarthy's home:

> Having me there was like having a dog present who had been trained to say a few words but overcome with inadequacy had forgotten them. Well, toward morning the conversation turned on the Eucharist, which I, being the Catholic, was obviously supposed to defend. She [Mary McCarthy] said when she was a child and received the Host, she thought of it as the Holy Ghost, He being the "most portable" person of the Trinity; now she thought of it as a symbol and implied that it was a pretty good one. I then said, in a very shaky voice, "Well, if it's a symbol, to hell with it." That was all the defense I was capable of but I realize now that this is all I will ever be able to say

about it, outside of a story, except that it is the center
of existence for me; all the rest of life is expendable.

If Jesus is risen only because he lives on in our memories,
he is only a symbol; then "to hell with him" would be an
appropriate response. The risen Lord has to be identical
with Jesus of Nazareth, or our faith is vain. We Christians
must be a people wedded to history and, more specifically,
to the historical Jesus. Jesus, the Galilean Jewish prophet, is
the bedrock of our faith; without him and faith in his resurrection we build our lives and our religion on sand.
Hence, the importance of trying to get to know him as a
historical person.

It is not easy for us to experience Jesus as a real, historical human being, and the difficulty stems from our
upbringing and training. We did not start with an experience of a human being who was a member of our
extended family, a neighbor, a fellow student, a flesh-and-
blood preacher, as did the people who surrounded Jesus of
Nazareth. The first time we heard about Jesus he was
already removed from ordinary human experience. We
were taught to bow our heads when pronouncing his
name, to genuflect when we came into his presence. The
word *God*, with all its overtones of awe and immensity,
was intimately associated with the name of Jesus. I doubt
that many of us could have imagined Jesus as a boy and
young man like ourselves. I recall preachers and retreat
directors, for example, who said that Jesus' agony in the
garden was caused by his knowledge of all the sins that
would be committed for centuries to come. Is that kind of
knowledge human? I also recall preachers saying that
Jesus' sufferings had been the worst sufferings ever experienced by a human being; and I recall doubting it since he
was God and knew that it would all turn out well in the
end. Besides, I had been taught that Jesus enjoyed the

beatific vision from the womb. Karl Rahner correctly opined that most Christians hold the view: "Wasn't it good of the good God to come down to earth looking like a human being?" Much of what preachers and theologians told us about Jesus would lead to such a view. We could, of course, mouth the orthodox line that Jesus is both fully human and fully divine, but we predicated things of Jesus that, in effect, denied him real humanity. If, for example, Jesus knew with absolute certitude, when he chose him, that Judas would betray him, then he was not really human. We find it hard to experience Jesus as a real, historical human being, therefore, because we are part of a tradition that has assumed a notion of God and applied it to Jesus. In an article in *Bible Review* N. T. Wright notes:

> Western orthodoxy has for too long had an overly lofty, detached and oppressive view of God. It has always tended to approach christology by assuming this view of God, and trying to fit Jesus into it. The result has been a docetic Jesus—that is, a Jesus who only seems to be truly human, but in fact is not. My proposal is not that we know what the word "God" means, and manage somehow to fit Jesus into that. Instead, I suggest that we think historically about a young Jew, possessed of a desperately risky, indeed apparently crazy, vocation, riding into Jerusalem, denouncing the Temple, dining once more with his friends, and dying on a Roman cross—and that we somehow allow our meaning of the word "God" to be re-centered on that point.

As the Letter to the Hebrews says: "For we do not have a high priest who is unable to sympathize with our weaknesses, but we have one who in every respect has been tested as we are, yet without sin" (Heb 4:15). To experience the humanity of Jesus we need to begin, not with a notion of God, but with human experience and with as much historical knowledge as we can get.

In *Who Do You Say I Am?* I made use of the first two of a promised three volumes of John Meier's *A Marginal Jew: Rethinking the Historical Jesus* to help readers to move toward a closer relationship with the historical Jesus. In the meantime I have read N. T. Wright's first two volumes of a work whose overall title is *Christian Origins and the Question of God.* Wright's two volumes have had a profound effect on my own relation with Jesus and have reordered my thinking about the whole New Testament period. Without going into the details of Wright's comprehensive and immensely scholarly work, I want to present a summary of what we can, with some degree of historical accuracy, say about the historical Jesus. My purpose is to help the reader to move toward a relation of greater intimacy with Jesus.

A Jew named Yeshua (Jesus) was born between 7 and 4 B.C. He grew up as part of a rather large extended family in Nazareth. His own name and the names in his family, Miryam (Mary) and Yosef (Joseph), Jacob (James), Judah (Jude) and Simon, were associated with early Israelite history, the time of the patriarchs, the Exodus to and conquest of the promised land. That the family used such names might indicate that they shared in the reawakening in Galilee of the yearning for the restoration of the glory days of Israel when Yahweh dwelt with his people. His putative father, Yosef, was considered to be of David's lineage. Jesus might have grown up, therefore, with a sense that he was of David's line and heard the stories of David and the promises to David from that vantage point. Like us, therefore, he would have been influenced in the formation of his identity by the stories he heard about his family and its history.

Nazareth was a small village in southern Galilee, a fertile area studded with small hamlets and villages clustered around small and large cities. Jesus learned woodworking, the trade of his father, and probably did not have much formal schooling. His own language was Aramaic, with a distinctive Galilean dialect. (Apparently, bystanders knew that Peter was a Galilean because of his accent; cf. Lk 22:59.) Those of us who speak our own language with a provincial accent have something in common with Jesus of Galilee. He knew Hebrew and probably some Greek since there were a number of Greek-speaking people in the area. Galilee was known as Galilee of the Nations because so many non-Jews lived there. As a result of the close proximity of so many non-Jews and the threat to Jewish identity occasioned by such closeness, Galilean Jews had an uncomplicated type of piety. For them, according to volume 2 of Meier,

> ...fidelity to the Jewish religion meant fidelity to the basics spelled out in the Mosaic Law: circumcision, observance of the Sabbath, observance of kosher food laws, and pilgrimage to the Jerusalem temple, whose sacrificial ritual during the great feasts was the high point of the annual cycle of their religious life. Surrounded as they were by a fair number of Gentiles and a fair amount of Hellenistic culture...,these Galilean Jews of the countryside would cling tenaciously to the basics of their religion as "boundary symbols" reinforcing their identity.

Jesus was formed in this culture. If we have any sense of what it is like to grow up in an atmosphere like this, we can have empathy with him. Those of us, like myself, who grew up in a kind of "ghetto Catholic culture" during the depression days before World War II can appreciate some of the features of

Jesus' upbringing in spite of the very obvious differences that
centuries make. I did not have much contact with non-
Catholics, for example, and lived in a relatively tight-knit,
closed environment. And I was taught in Catholic schools to
take pride in our distinctiveness as Catholics.

Jesus grew up in this family context, in this area of Israel
and in this culture. Here he learned the story of his people
and engaged in the practices that made their worldview
second nature. He learned to pray through the liturgies in
which he participated at home, in the synagogue and in
the temple during the yearly pilgrimages to Jerusalem.
Jesus prayed the same psalms we prayed in the early chapters of this book. He heard the same stories of Yahweh's
love for Israel, of Yahweh's desire for intimate union with
them, which we read. Jesus of Nazareth, like us, was made
for union with God and would have found in the Hebrew
scriptures of his people prayers that expressed the longing
of his heart. Jesus would have yearned for the same union
with Yahweh, would have yearned for the day of the Lord,
the day when Yahweh would bring about what he wants
with his world. In other words, he, too, yearned for the
Peaceable Kingdom. Already we have the beginning of an
entrée to knowing Jesus better. Because God desires Jesus
into existence, his own deepest desire is for union with
God. We can approach him with questions we might have
about our own desire for God. We can ask Jesus how he
prayed and whether he felt the same resistance to the
desire for union with God that we often feel.

We can also talk with him about the joys and trials of
being part of a particular family and ethnic group. How
did he deal with the likes and dislikes, the resentments
and petty upsets that accompany being part of any family
or close-linked group of people? Did he find some of his
relatives embarrassing? It would seem that some of his
family thought he was crazy at one point of his ministry

("When his family heard it, they went out to restrain him, for people were saying, 'He has gone out of his mind'" Mk 3:21). Recall that Nazareth was a small village where there were few secrets. Probably they were embarrassed about him. How did he deal with such incidents so common in family life? What was his reaction to his own anger? to the anger of others to him? What was it like for him to grow up in a country occupied by a foreign army? How much did the Roman occupiers impinge on his life? Did he see any of the sometimes purposeful, sometimes random cruelty that usually accompanies any army of occupation, which has little appreciation of a different culture and, perhaps, some fear of the subjugated people? For example, did Jesus see young men being pressed into service to carry loads for the Roman occupiers (perhaps the basis for his remark about going the extra mile in his instruction to his followers)? In his early years was he afraid of the Romans? Did he share some of the resentment of his family, friends and neighbors against the burdensome taxes of Herod? Did he yearn for freedom from Herod's and the Romans' rule? Becoming aware that Jesus of Nazareth was a real human being like us opens up many areas for conversation and mutual transparency.

Jesus must have been a keen observer as he grew up. During his public life he used many images from ordinary life. These images can help us to know him better: he saw shepherds seeking lost sheep, a woman seeking a lost coin, men strewing seed, women in labor and other everyday scenes. He knew how farmers depend on rain and sun and delighted in the birds of the air and the lilies of the fields. We can contemplate the images used in the gospels to get some sense of the kind of man Jesus was. We can also talk with him about the things we observe and enjoy.

Jesus as a young man chose not to marry and have children. This was, in his time, an unusual, but not unheard of choice; John the Baptist seems also to have made the same choice. Jesus was fully human with the sexual drive of a male. How did he deal with the sexual urges of adolescence and young adulthood? In his culture men were expected to marry and have children. He came to believe that his vocation precluded marriage and family. How did he come to make this decision? Even after making it he had to deal with the normal desires of any human being. Thus we can speak with Jesus about our common gendered and sexual nature. We can learn to discuss with him this most private part of our lives.

Because he was born into this world, he grew up in a family and a culture that shaped him, just as we grew up in a family and a culture that shaped us. He imbibed a worldview that conditioned how he saw the world around him, just as we did, and this worldview operated in him as it does in us, outside our conscious awareness for the most part. A worldview answers the basic questions of existence for those who share in it: Who are we? Where are we? What's the problem? What's the solution? What time is it? A worldview is the lens through which we comprehend our world. Like the lenses many of us use to help our sight, a worldview is taken for granted and operates without our awareness unless something happens that causes us to reflect on it. In the United States, for example, we imbibed a worldview after World War II that could be expressed in this way: Who are we? We are a God-blessed, freedom-loving, democratic people. Where are we? We are in the land of the free, a land of opportunity. What's wrong? There are enemies without and within, namely, the Soviet Union and the forces of worldwide Communism, who are bent on our destruction and the conquest of the world. What's the solution? We must defeat them and thwart them at every turn. What time is it? The time of great trial of all free peoples. To remind us of how our worldview colors everything we see, understand and do, let me cite a paragraph from John Staudenmeier, a U.S. Jesuit writing to his fellow Jesuits:

> In recent years I have grown in the conviction that I do not best understand myself as a believer who tries to love and engage his culture. The wiser question asks, Since it is a given that I am shaped by my culture, what do I need to help me to become a believer? I never possess faith as some fully formed object that I then bring to my culture. In faith I live a lifelong conversion of the culture I carry within me.
>
> I am, in short, a late-twentieth-century capitalist; along with most of the readers of this essay, I carry the inclinations, the burdens, the nobilities, and the violences of capitalist culture deeply etched in the core of my being. My situation is no worse, surely, than that of citizens of other cultures. But no better either. Culture lies too deeply embedded in human beings to ever become completely baptized, and the life of faith in every era takes the form of a holy tension between primordial cultural tendencies and God's endlessly affectionate challenge to learn to live faithfully.

Jesus was no different than Staudenmeier or any of us in being impacted by his culture and its worldview. As a result he would also have had the narrowness of vision and prejudices of that worldview and could only learn to overcome them through experience.

Wright pieces together the elements of the worldview of the Israelites of Jesus' time. It was the period called the "Second Temple," the time after the destruction of the first Temple and the Babylonian captivity. The destruction of the temple by the Babylonians was a national catastrophe etched into the memories of every Jew since that time.

Work on rebuilding the temple began in the late sixth century B.C. Herod the Great began remodeling and expanding it just before Jesus was born. Many Jews of the period, however, did not believe that he was the right king, or that God had fulfilled his promise to make his dwelling with them in this restored temple. According to Wright in volume 1 of *Christian Origins and the Question of God,* these are the elements of the worldview shared by the Jewish people in terms of the five questions that are implicitly addressed in all worldviews.

1. Who are we? We are Israel, the chosen people of the creator god.

2. Where are we? We are in the holy land, focused on the Temple, but, paradoxically, we are still in exile.

3. What is wrong? We have the wrong rulers: pagans on the one hand, compromised Jews on the other, or, halfway between, Herod and his family. We are all involved in a less-than-ideal situation.

4. What is the solution? Our god must act again to give us the true sort of rule, that is, his own kingship exercised through properly appointed officials (a true priesthood; possibly a true king); and in the meantime Israel must be faithful to his covenant charter.

The worldview also answered the fifth question, "What time is it?" in this way: "It is very close to the time of Yahweh's coming." Jews of the period differed on the details. For example, the Essenes believed that they were the real Israel, just as Jesus would teach his followers that they were the real Israel. But in principle, Wright believes, these answers constituted the worldview of Jesus' era and were expressed in stories, in symbols and in civic and religious practices.

The story they told themselves ran something like this: God created a universe that was good, but the first man and woman disobeyed their creator and introduced sin and death into the world. God, however, acted to put things right by choosing, against all odds, the people of Israel, through their patriarch Abraham, to be his chosen people. We have become so used to hearing this story that we easily miss the astonishing boldness of the claim that the creator of the universe had chosen this small, stiff-necked, nomadic racial group to be his special people. Even more astonishingly their story said that they were chosen not just for their good, but also for the good of the whole world. Through them God would undo the evil introduced into the world by the sin of the first human beings and the subsequent sins of human beings. Jesus grew up with this story; he was a part of it; it made him who he was.

The creator, whom they called Yahweh, acted decisively to free this people from slavery in Egypt and made a covenant with them in the desert through Moses. Yahweh dwelt with them in their wanderings in the desert, and when he brought them into the Promised Land, he continued to dwell with them in the Ark of the Covenant and finally in the temple built by Solomon. Yahweh had also given Moses the Torah, the Law, by which they were to live. In addition, in this period after the exile in Babylon the issue of who was a Jew, a member of the chosen people, that is, the issue of racial identity, was a burning one because of the dangers of assimilation. Thus, the four vital symbols of Yahweh's covenantal love are the land, the temple, Torah and racial identity. These were, therefore, the sacred symbols of Jesus' worldview.

Yahweh had never repented of his covenant, but Israel had often been unfaithful to the covenant and suffered grievously as a result. National catastrophes were interpreted by Israel's prophets as signs that because of

Israel's sins Yahweh had withdrawn his saving presence for a time. For example, at the time of the Babylonian captivity the prophet Ezekiel, in a vision, saw Yahweh's presence leave the temple (Ez 10:1–5, 15–22). Through it all Yahweh continued to assert his fidelity to the covenant and promised to be with Israel. Faithful Jews expected that Yahweh's presence would return to the land and the temple. One of the reasons why, in the time of Jesus, they still felt in exile in spite of the refurbishing of the temple by Herod the Great was that God's presence was not palpably present in that extraordinarily beautiful building. At this time the expectation that God would soon return was very high.

The story was learned not only through repeated telling but also through civic and religious practices, especially through prayer, liturgy, study of Torah and the keeping of kosher. Those of us who grew up in a Catholic "culture" will have an opening to conversation with Jesus about his practices by recalling the novenas, the processions, First Fridays, the Lenten fasts, the abstinence from meat on Friday and other such practices that set us apart and told us who we were. In addition, every male Jew carried on his body the sign of belonging to this covenanted people, circumcision.

Jesus was a man immersed in this culture with its implicit worldview and its story. He looked at his world through the lens provided to him by this culture. If he came to challenge that worldview, as indeed he did, it was as an insider, not as an outsider. He was a Galilean Jewish woodworker of the first century of our era. He was not a noble or sophisticated Greek or Roman. Still less was he a twentieth-century citizen of the United States. If we want to know Jesus of Nazareth, then, it will be a help to know something of his time and culture.

It was in this culture that Jesus discovered his vocation

as a prophet and as the Messiah. It is clear that he was a religious genius who knew his people's story and its heroes very well. He seems to have based his ministry on the ministry of the great prophets of Israel. He also seems to have had as mentor John the Baptist, the prophet who practiced a baptism of repentance in the desert area of the lower Jordan. John preached powerful sermons about the imminent coming of God to judge Israel. He called on all to repent and to be baptized by himself, thus making himself and his ministry key to salvation. At the same time he spoke of someone who was to come after him, the "stronger one" who would baptize with the Holy Spirit (Lk 3:16). Jesus was baptized by John, and this event clearly signaled the beginning of a new life for Jesus. Wright believes that it was at the moment of his baptism "that Jesus received either the call to act as Israel's Messiah, or, supposing he had already been aware of such a call, confirmation of this vocation" *(Jesus and the Victory of God)*. Throughout his ministry Jesus remained indebted to John and spoke admiringly of him. At the same time Jesus obviously went beyond John both in his teaching and in his style of ministry and life. For example, unlike John, Jesus had a wandering ministry, gave extensive teachings and performed many marvelous healings. Hence Jesus had to come to terms with the tension between loyalty to his mentor and loyalty to his own call and discernment. Here again we have food for thought and prayer as we try to become more intimate with Jesus. How did he come to a sense of his vocation? Did the notion gradually develop or was he suddenly seized with the conviction that he had a special calling? What was this experience at his baptism like? I have often asked Jesus to remind me of any comparable experiences that might let me have an inkling of his call. Indeed, the writing of this book has been the occasion for many such questions and some surprising reminders. As I indicated earlier in this chapter, the best entrée to an intimate relationship with Jesus is through our own experience. We trust that the Spirit will enlighten us as we pray to know Jesus more intimately in order to love him more ardently and to follow him more closely.

Chapter 10

The Ministry of Jesus

As we begin this second chapter on intimacy with Jesus, we remind ourselves that we are seeking to know Jesus better in order to love him more deeply and follow him more closely. We want a relationship of reciprocal intimacy. Hence we ask that he reveal himself to us just as, we presume, he wants us to reveal ourselves to him. In this chapter we will look at the ministry of Jesus, a ministry that eventually led him to Jerusalem and his death.

Like John, Jesus preached the imminent coming of Yahweh to rule and called his hearers to repentance. Unlike John, who gathered crowds at the Jordan, Jesus carried on his prophetic ministry as a wanderer in Galilee. "And Jesus said to him, 'Foxes have holes, and birds of the air have nests; but the Son of Man has nowhere to lay his head'" (Mt 8:20). He went around the villages and small towns of Galilee and crossed over the Jordan into the non-Jewish region called the Decapolis. In the course of this ministry he would obviously have repeated stories and sayings many times with variations called for by the circumstances of the new audience. Thus we have one reason for some of the variations in the stories and sayings in the gospels. We sense in the gospels that his ministry was urgent. There was little time to spare before the day of judgment. "Now after John was arrested, Jesus came to Galilee, proclaiming the good news of God, and saying, 'The time is fulfilled, and the kingdom of God has come near; repent, and believe in the good news'" (Mk 1:14–15).

As he moved around, Jesus gathered small groups of disciples, to whom he taught a way of life and a special prayer, the Our Father. One distinctive feature of the lifestyle of Jesus' followers was that they did not fast, as did the disciples of John and of the Pharisees. In small villages where there were no secrets such lifestyles were noticed and commented on. "Now John's disciples and the Pharisees were fasting; and people came and said to him, 'Why do John's disciples and the disciples of the Pharisees fast, but your disciples do not fast?'" (Mk 2:18)

Jesus taught his disciples that they were the real people of God, whose source of cohesion was their allegiance to Jesus himself. Most of these disciples stayed in their villages, but others followed Jesus in his itinerant ministry. From among these he chose twelve to be his closest disciples. This choice of twelve is significant, for by this symbolic action Jesus indicated that he was reconstituting Israel. These twelve represented the twelve tribes of Israel. Jesus' disciples were, therefore, the true Israel, and the lifestyle and prayer he taught them was the one needed for this time of God's coming to rule. What kind of man is this prophet who does what Yahweh himself did in choosing the twelve tribes as his special people? Because we are so conditioned by our training to think of Jesus as God, we have to remind ourselves continually that he was also truly a human being like us in all things (save sin). What did it mean for this man to become aware of such a unique vocation? Perhaps we have an inkling in our own experience of being awed by our own call, or our own gifts; for example, the awe of becoming the father or mother of a child, or the awe of knowing that my words have been a channel of God's grace for another.

Before we look at the lifestyle he taught his disciples, we need to look at the message he proclaimed in word and deed. Central to his preaching is the rule or kingdom of God. Jesus did not invent this phrase; his hearers would recognize it. It would conjure up in them prophecies of God's coming to rule with power to save his people from their enemies, to end their exile, to forgive their sins, to dwell with them forever in "shalom," peace. But most of his hearers expected that this coming of God would mean victory in battle over the occupying armies, the cleansing of the temple from the impurities occasioned by pagan occupation and the onset of God's rule in justice and right-eousness over the whole world. Some believed that God's coming to rule would require an armed uprising against the hated Roman occupiers.

Jesus' telling of the story of God's coming to reign was subversive. He believed that an armed uprising against the Romans would be madness and contrary to Yahweh's wishes. He warned over and over again against such folly. Jesus' warnings came to a head when he rode down the Mount of Olives, burst into tears as he saw the beautiful city and said:

> "If you, even you, had only recognized on this day the things that make for peace! But now they are hidden from your eyes. Indeed, the days will come upon you, when your enemies will set up ramparts around you and surround you, and hem you in on every side. They will crush you to the ground, you and your children within you, and they will not leave within you one stone upon another; because you did not recognize the time of your visitation from God." (Lk 19:42–44)

Jesus, like Jeremiah before him, saw that the stubborn insistence on the protection of the temple and on the use of arms would lead to destruction. And like Jeremiah and the other prophets, he announced the coming catastrophe as punishment from Yahweh on his people. Thus Jesus' proclamation of the coming of God's rule through his ministry was a direct attack on the position of the majority party of the Pharisees and ran counter to what most people expected would happen when God finally came to rule.

If God's coming to rule would not come about through armed uprising, how would it happen? We get some inkling in the practices Jesus inculcated in his followers.

> "Blessed are the poor in spirit, for theirs is the kingdom of heaven....Blessed are the peacemakers, for they will be called children of God. Blessed are those who are persecuted for righteousness' sake, for theirs is the kingdom of heaven." (Mt 5:3, 9–10)

> "You have heard that it was said, 'An eye for an eye and a tooth for a tooth.' But I say to you, Do not resist an evildoer. But if anyone strikes you on the right cheek, turn the other also; and if anyone wants to sue you and take your coat, give your cloak as well; and if anyone forces you to go one mile, go also the second mile. Give to everyone who begs from you, and do not refuse anyone who wants to borrow from you.

> "You have heard that it was said, 'You shall love your neighbor and hate your enemy.' But I say to you, Love your enemies and pray for those who persecute you, so that you may be children of your Father in heaven; for he makes his sun rise on the evil and on the good, and sends rain on the righteous and on the unrighteous." (Mt 5:38–45)

We have to take these sayings in their historical context. Jesus tells people who have prized possession of the land as a sign of God's love not to be concerned about ownership of property; the poor are blessed and will inherit the kingdom of God. He tells an oppressed and occupied people to turn the other cheek when the occupier gives them the back of the hand. Thus they look the oppressor in the eye and open themselves to another slap in the face; this would be the act of a free person, but not a violent response to the initial insult. If the Roman soldier orders you to carry his baggage one mile, go two miles. To a people conditioned to feuding and who remembered grudges for generations, he says "Love your enemies." God's kingdom will not come through violence but through self-sacrificing love. Indeed, the most subversive aspect of these sayings may be the last one; the implication is that all people are God's children, not just the chosen people. This idea, of course, is implicit in the belief of the Israelites that Yahweh, their God, is the one God, the one creator of the universe. Through his prayer and reflection Jesus has come to a subversive version of Israel's story. To get some inkling of the process of his conversion to this version we need to reflect on our own journey from childhood to adulthood and the changes in our worldview that happened along the way. If you have come to a version of what it means to be a Christian that differs from the one you imbibed growing up, then you have some idea of what happened to Jesus.

This leads us to another aspect of Jesus' lifestyle, both his own and the one he encouraged in his followers, namely, his open table fellowship.

And as he sat at dinner in Levi's house, many tax collectors and sinners were also sitting with Jesus and his disciples—for there were many who followed him. When the scribes of the Pharisees saw that he was eating with sinners and tax collectors, they said to his disciples, "Why does he eat with tax collectors and sinners?" When Jesus heard this, he said to them, "Those who are well have no need of a physician, but those who are sick; I have come to call not the righteous but sinners." (Mk 2:15–17)

Tax collectors in Galilee were not working directly for Rome, but for Herod Antipas. They seem to have been hated because they extorted money from people and enriched themselves. "Sinners" were those who deliberately flouted the Law, among them prostitutes. With these "sinners," among others, Jesus ate and drank, and in doing so, was offering them "forgiveness of sins." (He also ate with Pharisees, when invited, by the way.) In Jesus' time, forgiveness of sins was associated with the coming of Yahweh to rule. The people of God knew that they had been sent into exile because of their sins. As long as they were in exile, they were still in their sins, and in Jesus' time, as we saw, they still felt in exile. Second Isaiah opens with the words of comfort that signaled the end of Israel's exile. "Comfort, O comfort my people, says your God. Speak tenderly to Jerusalem, and cry to her that she has served her term, that her penalty is paid, that she has received from the Lord's hand double for all her sins" (Is 40:1–2). If Jesus was offering forgiveness of sins and inviting sinners to eat and drink with him, then he was announcing with word and action that the exile was coming to an end with his ministry.

Obviously some of his enemies realized very well what he was doing and objected strongly. Jesus took issue with them by contrasting his own ministry with that of John the Baptist.

"But to what will I compare this generation? It is like children sitting in the marketplaces and calling to one another, 'We played the flute for you, and you did not dance; we wailed, and you did not mourn.' For John came neither eating nor drinking, and they say, 'He has a demon'; the Son of Man came eating and drinking, and they say, 'Look, a glutton and a drunkard, a friend of tax collectors and sinners!' Yet wisdom is vindicated by her deeds." (Mt 11:16–19)

Clearly Jesus' practice of table fellowship was such as to cause talk among the people. But the issue with the Pharisees was not that they were legalists while Jesus was offering God's love and forgiveness. Rather, as Wright points out in *Jesus and the Victory of God:*

> The point is that *Jesus was offering the return from exile, the renewed covenant, the eschatological 'forgiveness of sins'*—in other words, the kingdom of god. And he was offering this final eschatological blessing outside the official structures, to all the wrong people, and on his own authority. This was his real offense.

Jesus' table fellowship was part of his prophetic messianic ministry. And he enjoined the same kind of fellowship on his followers who were the renewed people of God, the real Israel. As we contemplate Jesus in these actions, what does he tell us about our following of him? Jesus can be an uncomfortable friend.

The story of the feeding of a multitude on the shore of the Sea of Galilee appears in all four gospels, the only miracle to do so. Jesus must have celebrated at least one memorable meal of bread and fish in a setting that spoke powerfully of the messianic banquet promised by the prophets. The prophet Isaiah had promised:

On this mountain the Lord of hosts will make for all
peoples a feast of rich food, a feast of well-aged
wines, of rich food filled with marrow, of well-aged
wines strained clear. And he will destroy on this
mountain the shroud that is cast over all peoples, the
sheet that is spread over all nations; he will swallow
up death forever. Then the Lord God will wipe away
the tears from all faces, and the disgrace of his people
he will take away from all the earth, for the Lord has
spoken. It will be said on that day, Lo, this is our God;
we have waited for him, so that he might save us. This
is the Lord for whom we have waited; let us be glad
and rejoice in his salvation. (Is 25:6–9)

Jesus knew of such prophecies and, it seems, consciously
evoked them through his actions and words. At this meal
or these meals by the Sea of Galilee, thousands seem to
have been fed by a miracle, and there were abundant left-
overs. We need to realize, however, that this banquet or
these banquets took place in the open. No one could possibly check the identities of those who were invited to partic-
ipate. It is clearly possible that non-Jews took part. Surely
tax collectors and sinners of various kinds enjoyed the
meal. Jesus was, indeed, inviting the wrong kinds of
people into his messianic banquet. Mind you, Jesus was
not a "live-and-let-live" modern "liberal" for whom it does
not matter what kind of life one leads. He demanded
repentance of sinners. What got him into trouble was that
he offered forgiveness of sins on his own authority and did
not require temple sacrifice and ritual cleansing prior to
the forgiveness. He seems to have believed that people
would change their attitudes and behaviors through close
contact with him. The same thing can happen to us if we
continue to develop our relationship with him.

Jesus was not only mighty in word, but also mighty in

deed. There is no way of getting around the fact that Jesus thought of himself as a wonder worker and was so considered by the people of his time. In fact, after he raised the son of the widow of Nain from the dead, we read:

> Fear seized all of them; and they glorified God, saying, "A great prophet has risen among us!" and "God has looked favorably on his people!" This word about him spread throughout Judea and all the surrounding country. The disciples of John reported all these things to him. So John summoned two of his disciples and sent them to the Lord to ask, "Are you the one who is to come, or are we to wait for another?" When the men had come to him, they said, "John the Baptist has sent us to you to ask, 'Are you the one who is to come, or are we to wait for another?'" Jesus had just then cured many people of diseases, plagues, and evil spirits, and had given sight to many who were blind. And he answered them, "Go and tell John what you have seen and heard: the blind receive their sight, the lame walk, the lepers are cleansed, the deaf hear, the dead are raised, the poor have good news brought to them. And blessed is anyone who takes no offense at me." (Lk 7:16–23)

Jesus did not perform these mighty deeds to prove that he was the Messiah. Rather, with them he was demonstrating in action that God's rule was indeed at hand, as the prophets had promised. For the prophets these healings would restore to membership in the chosen people those who had been excluded as ritually unclean or otherwise marginal. When Jesus healed the blind, the dumb, the leper, he was announcing in action the coming of God to rule in much the same way as he announced this coming by his open table fellowship. In *Jesus and the Victory of God*, Wright puts it this way:

> In other words, these healings, at the deepest level of understanding on the part of Jesus and his contemporaries, would be seen as part of his total ministry, specifically, part of that open welcome which went with the inauguration of the kingdom—and, consequently, part of his subversive work, which was likely to get him into trouble.

In addition, Jesus' actions in many of these cures broke some taboos. He touched lepers, for example, and the woman with the hemorrhage; he laid his hand on the corpse of the widow's son and of the daughter of Jairus. With these actions he declared that these persons were not unclean. No wonder that the people were astounded and said "We have never seen anything like this!" (Mk 2:12). We who want to know Jesus better can also be astounded at the kind of human being he is and the kind of authority he claims. And remember that he was a human being like us in all things save sin.

Jesus confounded his hearers and even his own family by maintaining that allegiance to him took precedence over blood ties. In Mark's gospel, after the scenes where Jesus' own family thought him mad and the religious leaders accused him of being possessed by a demon, we read:

> Then his mother and his brothers came; and standing outside, they sent to him and called him. A crowd was sitting around him; and they said to him, "Your mother and your brothers and sisters are outside, asking for you." And he replied, "Who are my mother and my brothers?" And looking at those who sat

around him, he said, "Here are my mother and my brothers! Whoever does the will of God is my brother and sister and mother." (Mk 3:31–35)

In his culture such a statement would have been shocking. In effect, he made loyalty to himself, not blood ties, the criterion of belonging to the new Israel. Once in a retreat a young man was contemplating this scene. He became part of the events and saw the people Jesus meant as his brothers and sisters and mother; among them were many people the young man did not like. It was instructive for him to realize that Jesus was very serious about who were his brothers and sisters.

Even more shocking was the following response. "To another he said, 'Follow me.' But he said, 'Lord, first let me go and bury my father.' But Jesus said to him, 'Let the dead bury their own dead; but as for you, go and proclaim the kingdom of God'" (Lk 9:59–60). Here Jesus takes it upon himself to say that obedience to him takes precedence over obedience to the Law and to the most sacred obligation of family ties. The new Israel would be defined by ties to him before all else. This Galilean Jew had a unique sense of his vocation. At the same time, we have to know that any number of would-be messiahs and Jewish leaders of his era also made claims that allegiance to themselves constituted the real Israel. Jesus is a first-century Jew making extraordinary claims about himself and his ministry. A human being like us....

Jesus had a wonderful imagination. He told stories of lost sheep, lost coins, lamps on a lamp stand, sowers in a field, and all these stories made a point about God's kingdom, his own ministry and the need for repentance. They were also deeply subversive of the worldview he grew up with. We have already noted how he told the marvelous story of the prodigal son in response to complaints by the Pharisees and

scribes about his table fellowship. At one level it is a beautiful story illustrating God's prodigal love for the sinner. But,
as we saw in chapter 5, Jesus used this story to tell his hearers that with his ministry God's rule was now present and
that the nitpickers and carpers were in danger of missing
the unique moment for which Israel had been pining and
about which the great prophets had spoken.

In the same way he told the story of the vineyard owner
in response to the chief priests and elders of the people who
asked him, "By what authority are you doing these things,
and who gave you this authority?" (Mt 21:23). He told it as
Israel's story, but with a subversive twist. The opening
words of the parable echo the parable of Isaiah where
Israel is compared to a vineyard. "Let me sing for my
beloved my love-song concerning his vineyard: My beloved
had a vineyard on a very fertile hill. He dug it and cleared
it of stones, and planted it with choice vines; he built a
watchtower in the midst of it, and hewed out a wine vat in
it; he expected it to yield grapes, but it yielded wild grapes"
(Is 5:1–2). In the face of fierce opposition Jesus says:

> "Listen to another parable. There was a landowner
> who planted a vineyard, put a fence around it, dug a
> wine press in it, and built a watchtower. Then he
> leased it to tenants and went to another country.
> When the harvest time had come, he sent his slaves to
> the tenants to collect his produce. But the tenants
> seized his slaves and beat one, killed another, and
> stoned another. Again he sent other slaves, more than
> the first; and they treated them in the same way.
> Finally he sent his son to them, saying, 'They will
> respect my son.' But when the tenants saw the son,
> they said to themselves, 'This is the heir; come, let us
> kill him and get his inheritance.' So they seized him,
> threw him out of the vineyard, and killed him. Now

when the owner of the vineyard comes, what will he do to those tenants?" They said to him, "He will put those wretches to a miserable death, and lease the vineyard to other tenants who will give him the produce at the harvest time." Jesus said to them, "Have you never read in the scriptures: 'The stone that the builders rejected has become the cornerstone; this was the Lord's doing, and it is amazing in our eyes'? Therefore I tell you, the kingdom of God will be taken away from you and given to a people that produces the fruits of the kingdom. The one who falls on this stone will be broken to pieces; and it will crush anyone on whom it falls." (Mt 21:33–43)

Jesus is telling the story of Israel, but he makes himself the central character of Israel's story. With him the story has reached its climax. The die is cast; even though they kill him, still he and his version of Israel's story will be vindicated. Again, we have to remind ourselves that the Jesus who came to this subversive version of Israel's story was a human being like us and a Jew of his time.

Another aspect of Jesus' ministry should engage our attention because it brings to the fore Jesus' recognition of who the real enemy of God's rule is. Jesus cast out demons and equated his power over the demons as a sign of God's coming to rule. "But if it is by the finger of God that I cast out the demons, then the kingdom of God has come to you" (Lk 11:20). The majority party of the Pharisees and, more than likely, most Jews of the time, saw the real enemy of Israel and, therefore, of God, as the pagans, and especially the Roman occupiers. Over and over again Jesus warned his hearers that the real enemy was Satan, the prince of darkness. Satan had seduced the Israelites as well as the pagans. In the desert Jesus faced this enemy and refused to use the strategies and means of the evil one to carry out his vocation (Lk 4:1–13). God's rule cannot come about through the means proposed by Satan, and among those means is an armed rebellion. Jesus, like any believing Jew, believed that God was acting in history to bring about his rule. (We might use the notion of "God's project" or "God's intention.") He also believed that God's enemy, Satan, was doing everything in his power to thwart God's actions. "Whoever is not against us is for us" (Mk 9:40). In volume 2 of *A Marginal Jew,* John Meier puts the matter this way:

> ...it is important to realize that, in the view of Jesus,...human beings were not basically neutral territories that might be influenced by divine or demonic forces now and then....human existence was seen as a battlefield dominated by one or the other supernatural force, God or Satan (alias Belial or the devil). A human being might have a part in choosing which "field of force" would dominate his or her life, i.e., which force he or she would choose to side with. But no human being was free to choose simply to be free of these supernatural forces. One was dominated by either one or the other, and to pass *from* one was necessarily to pass *into* the control of the other. At least over the long term, one could not maintain a neutral stance vis-à-vis God and Satan.

As we ask to know Jesus better in order to love him more deeply and to follow him more closely, we need to face the question he faced about the nature of the enemy of God. In our day there is a tendency to play down the role of the evil one. But the horrors this century has witnessed and continues to witness should give us pause. Jesus of Nazareth saw with absolute clarity that in his time the real enemy of God was Satan. Why should he not have continued his enmity even after his definitive defeat at Calvary?

Here then is Jesus' version of the story of Israel, his subversive version of Israel's worldview. Who are we? Those who follow me are the real people of God as light for the world. Where are we? We are in God's world, the whole of it God's vineyard. What's wrong? The evil one, Satan, has bewitched not only the pagans but also the Israelites. What is the solution? I am, and my way of being Messiah. What time is it? The time of crisis for Israel and the world. With his ministry Jesus has assembled the tinder around himself that only needs a spark to burst into flame. In the next chapter we shall see that he himself kindled the blaze.

As we contemplate the words and actions of the historical Jesus with the desire to know him more intimately in order to love him more deeply and follow him more closely, we find a young Jew with an awe-inspiringly unique sense of vocation, of commitment to God and what God intends through his ministry, and of clarity about his and Israel's destiny in God's plans for the world. What kind of human being is this? What does it mean to follow him more closely?

Chapter 11

Jesus' Last Week

Jesus, then, believed himself to be the focal point of the people of YHWH, the returned-from-exile people, the people of the renewed covenant, the people whose sins were now to be forgiven. He embodied what he had announced. He was the true interpreter of Torah; the true builder of the Temple; the true spokesperson for Wisdom....

Jesus' redefined notion of Messiahship...pointed to a fulfillment of Israel's destiny which no one had imagined or suspected. He came, as representative of the people of YHWH, to bring about the end of exile, the renewal of the covenant, the forgiveness of sins. To accomplish this, an obvious first-century option for a would-be Messiah would run: go to Jerusalem, fight the battle against the forces of evil, and get yourself enthroned as the rightful king. Jesus, in fact, adopted precisely this strategy. But, as he hinted to James and John, he had in mind a different battle, a different throne. It is to this dark theme that we must now turn. (N. T. Wright, *Jesus and the Victory of God*)

Thus does Wright set the stage for Jesus' entry into Jerusalem and the final week of his life. As we turn to "this dark theme," let us once again recall our desire to know him more intimately in order to love him more deeply and to follow him more closely. We remind ourselves that Jesus was a young Jew of the first century, a Jew of the first commandment. He became humanly conscious of himself and his relation to Yahweh that could well have led him to wonder about his own sanity. He, like us, had to discern whether the dreams, the insights and the intuitions he had were from God or not. My own growth in intimacy with Jesus has required a radical shift. As I have been forced to face more directly his Jewish humanity, I have had to be willing to face more openly and directly my own humanity as a son of Irish immigrants raised in the United States in a Catholic culture that has undergone a sea change during my lifetime. I have had to trust my intuitions in prayer in a way that I could not have done even twenty-five years ago. I have had to let go of presuppositions of what Jesus might have thought and felt as he faced his final week. Among other things that I have gained is a profound appreciation of his courage and faith as he lived out his vocation to its bitter end. Let us now turn to "this dark theme," asking to know Jesus more intimately.

Wright argues that Jesus deliberately went to Jerusalem to die, to take upon himself the terrible punishment that he saw surely coming upon his people because they had not known the time of their visitation. Jesus had lamented over Jerusalem: "Jerusalem, Jerusalem, the city that kills the prophets and stones those who are sent to it! How often have I desired to gather your children together as a hen gathers her brood under her wings, and you were not willing! See, your house is left to you, desolate" (Mt 23:37–39). Jesus uses the image of a mother hen protecting her brood of chicks in a barnyard fire. The hen may perish in the fire, but her chicks are safe. The image recalls a number of passages in the Hebrew scriptures where Yahweh is likened to a hen protecting her chicks; for example, "How precious is your steadfast love, O God! All people may take refuge in the shadow of your wings" (Ps 36:7). In this and other passages, Jesus alludes to his vocation to take upon himself the punishment of his people. There is, however, another startling allusion: Jesus takes on the role assigned to Yahweh in the Hebrew texts. What kind of human being is this?

In this final week of his earthly life Jesus followed the injunctions he enjoined on his followers. He turned the other cheek, walked the extra mile. He saw that the real enemy was not the Romans or Herod, but Satan, the enemy of the creator of the universe. In the desert, after his baptism by John, he had faced this enemy and had refused to take up his strategies. Now he would refuse them again and go to his death trusting in his "Abba" to bring about his kingdom. Seen as a historical fact about a historical human being like us, this scenario does seem crazy, does it not? What kind of human being is Jesus? "Who do you say I am?"

After some time of public ministry in which he announced his intentions and claims in a veiled way through somewhat enigmatic parables and prophetic words and actions, Jesus now believes that the time is ripe for the decisive battle for which he has been preparing all his life. He makes a very public entrance into Jerusalem with the crowds coming up for Passover. He knows the prophecy of Zechariah:

> Rejoice greatly, O daughter Zion! Shout aloud, O daughter Jerusalem! Lo, your king comes to you; triumphant and victorious is he, humble and riding on a donkey, on a colt, the foal of a donkey. He will cut off the chariot from Ephraim and the war horse from

Jerusalem; and the battle bow shall be cut off, and he shall command peace to the nations; his dominion shall be from sea to sea, and from the River to the ends of the earth. (Zec 9:9-10)

Jesus deliberately rides into Jerusalem on a donkey knowing that the crowds will understand that he is claiming to be the king prophesied. In addition, this action signals his belief that with his triumphal entrance Yahweh is returning to Zion. Again, we have to wonder at the consciousness of himself that Jesus must have had. Think of a monotheistic Jew of the first century, not of a twentieth-century Christian theologian. He does not have the categories of the latter in which to understand himself; he does not think in terms of "Three Persons in one God" or "Second Person of the Blessed Trinity." But he has a unique sense of his vocation and mission, and now in this last week of his life he acts openly in terms of that sense. No wonder he was accused of blasphemy by the high priest at his trial. Either you believe him, or you must think him a blasphemer or a madman.

After the entrance into Jerusalem, he enters the temple and cleans it out. Wright argues that Jesus intended this action as a symbolic destruction of the temple. In Jesus' eyes the temple was corrupt not only in the way it did business, but also in the way it served as the focal point for those who believed that armed resistance to the hated Romans would have the blessing and protection of Yahweh. Most New Testament scholars agree that with this action Jesus ignited the spark in the tinder that had already been piled up around him through his ministry. With this action he sealed his doom.

To understand the kind of animosity this action engendered we have to recall the outrage that spontaneously arises when someone deliberately desecrates one of the symbols that defines who we are as a people. Think of the rage in the United States created by people who burn the flag. Jesus had already redefined the other symbols of the Jewish worldview of his era. The land was not to be coveted, but voluntarily given up. The Law was redefined by Jesus' own teaching and practice, including his sitting loose to the way of keeping Sabbath. Identity as a member of the chosen people was redefined not according to blood ties, but according to allegiance to Jesus. With the symbolic destruction of the temple he redefined where God now dwelt, and it seems clear that he believed that God now dwelt in him. In each case, Jesus made himself the central symbol of the new Israel.

The next significant symbolic action he performed in this eventful week occurred in the upper room. Probably, as John's gospel indicates, this meal in the upper room took place the day before the official Passover of that year, but Jesus clearly intended it to be a Passover meal. The Passover meal tells the story of Israel, especially the story of the Exodus and the Covenant, and makes the story and these events present for those participating in the meal. For first-century Jews, it also symbolized the new coming of Yahweh to rule. As the leader of the meal Jesus retells the story, but he gives it a new and very surprising twist. It is as if he said: "God is coming to rule *now and in and through me, and specifically through my death on the cross.*"

> While they were eating, Jesus took a loaf of bread, and after blessing it he broke it, gave it to the disciples, and said, "Take, eat; this is my body." Then he took a cup, and after giving thanks he gave it to them, saying, "Drink from it, all of you; for this is my blood of the covenant, which is poured out for many for the forgiveness of sins." (Mt 26:26–28)

His action with the bread and the cup is a prophetic, symbolic action much like Jeremiah smashing the earthenware
jug to signify the destruction of Jerusalem (Jer 19:10–15),
or like Ezechiel taking a brick as a model of Jerusalem
under siege (Ez 4:1–3). "This bread *is* my body; this cup *is*
my blood," just as Jeremiah's jug and Ezechiel's brick *are*
Jerusalem. Jesus enacts his own death in this symbolic
action, and it is for the forgiveness of sins; he is saying that
with his death the long exile of Israel is over. With his rid-
ing into Jerusalem on a donkey, the cleansing of the temple and this Passover meal Jesus enacted the coming of
God to rule, the coming of the kingdom. What kind of
human being is this? "Who do you say I am?"

With these actions Jesus brought to clarity what had been
implicit in his words and actions earlier, namely, that he
was the Messiah who was inaugurating God's rule now. The
time is ripe, it seems. The gospels clearly indicate that Jesus
made this fateful trip to Jerusalem knowing and predicting
what lay in store for him. In this final week Jesus declared
himself openly and, it seems, dared the chief priests to take
a stand. They had no choice but to believe in him and his
way of being Messiah or to bring him to trial. By any stretch
of the imagination, it is easy to see why the Jewish leaders
who did not want to join Jesus' movement would accuse him
of leading the people astray, a capital offense.

With his actions upon entering Jerusalem, Jesus walked
into the lions' den. He paid dearly for them, and very
soon. Why did he do it? What were his intentions, as far as
we can reconstruct them historically? Wright argues con-
vincingly that Jesus saw himself as a prophet warning
Israel of the consequences of compromising with pagan-
ism. For Jesus, compromising with the pagans included
believing that one could defeat the pagans with their
weapons: "all who take the sword will perish by the sword"
(Mt 26:52). Jesus'

kingdom-announcement, like all truly Jewish king-
dom-announcements, came as the message of the one
true God, the God of Israel, in opposition to pagan
power, pagan gods, and pagan politics. But, unlike
the other kingdom-announcers of his time...Jesus
declared that the way to the kingdom was the way of
peace, the way of love, the way of the cross. Fighting
the battle of the kingdom with the enemy's weapons
meant that one had already lost it in principle, and
would soon lose it, and lose it terribly, in practice.
(N. T. Wright, *Jesus and the Victory of God*)

Jesus had decided that his vocation was to go ahead of
Israel and take upon himself the horrible punishment that
awaited Israel if she continued on her path of folly. Jesus
took upon himself the martyr tradition of Israel, a tradition that had shown itself relatively recently at the time of
the Maccabees. Recall the story of the old man Eleazar (2
Mc 6:18ff.) and of the mother with her seven sons (2 Mc
7:1ff.), both of which stories feature in our liturgies. This
martyr tradition went back at least to the prophecy of
Second Isaiah (Chs 40–55), with its promise that Yahweh
would bring his people back from exile and also with its
servant songs. Jesus identified himself and his coming sufferings with the sufferings of Israel. "Why did Jesus die?"
asks Wright. "Ultimately, because he believed it was his
vocation." In other words, it was not the early church that
first used the suffering servant songs of Isaiah to explain
what Jesus had accomplished. Jesus himself knew this tradition and believed that it was his vocation to bring victory
to Israel through his own suffering on the Roman cross.
Jesus knew, for instance, this song from Second Isaiah:

> He was despised and rejected by others; a man of suf-
> fering and acquainted with infirmity; and as one

from whom others hide their faces he was despised, and we held him of no account. Surely he has borne our infirmities and carried our diseases; yet we accounted him stricken, struck down by God, and afflicted. But he was wounded for our transgressions, crushed for our iniquities; upon him was the punishment that made us whole, and by his bruises we are healed. All we like sheep have gone astray; we have all turned to our own way, and the Lord has laid on him the iniquity of us all. He was oppressed, and he was afflicted, yet he did not open his mouth; like a lamb that is led to the slaughter, and like a sheep that before its shearers is silent, so he did not open his mouth. By a perversion of justice he was taken away. Who could have imagined his future? For he was cut off from the land of the living, stricken for the transgression of my people. They made his grave with the wicked and his tomb with the rich, although he had done no violence, and there was no deceit in his mouth. Yet it was the will of the Lord to crush him with pain. When you make his life an offering for sin, he shall see his offspring, and shall prolong his days; through him the will of the Lord shall prosper. Out of his anguish he shall see light; he shall find satisfaction through his knowledge. The righteous one, my servant, shall make many righteous, and he shall bear their iniquities. Therefore I will allot him a portion with the great, and he shall divide the spoil with the strong; because he poured out himself to death, and was numbered with the transgressors; yet he bore the sin of many, and made intercession for the transgressors. (Is 53:3–12)

Jesus believed that this was his vocation. In the upper room he symbolically enacted his death as the victory of

God, as the coming of God to rule, as the forgiveness of sins. What kind of human being is this who could have come to believe in this vocation? "Who do you say I am?"

Once again, we remind ourselves that Jesus was a Jew of the first century who believed as did his fellow Jews. He was a monotheist who believed that there was one God who created the world and had called Israel to be his people for the sake of the world. He believed that Israel was the true people of this one God, elected by God to be the light of the world. He believed in the coming of Israel's God to rule, which would be the real return from exile, the real return of Yahweh to Zion. "The difference between the beliefs of Jesus and those of thousands of other Jews of his day amounted simply to this: he believed, also, that all these things were coming true in and through himself" (N. T. Wright, *Jesus and the Victory of God*) and specifically through his death on a cross. He was a human being like us in all things save sin. He came to the conclusion that Israel's story was coming to its climax in him, and that his vocation was to die on a cross as *the* way for Yahweh to come to rule. When we ponder these facts without recourse to theories about his divinity, we can be staggered and awed by the audacity of the man. It is not at all difficult to imagine his family thinking him crazy and the religious leaders of Israel thinking him possessed by a devil. What does it mean to want to become an intimate of such a man? "Who do you say I am?"

As Wright notes, to speak of Jesus' vocation is not the same thing as to speak of Jesus' knowledge of his divinity. "Jesus did not…'know that he was God' in the same way that one knows one is male or female, hungry or thirsty, or that one ate an orange an hour ago. His 'knowledge' was of a more risky, but perhaps more significant, sort: like knowing one is loved. One cannot 'prove' it except by living by it." In other words, Jesus had to take the risk of faith that any human being takes when he discerns a vocation from God. But Jesus' vocation, as he saw it, included within it actions that Yahweh had reserved to himself. Jesus, by entering Jerusalem on a donkey, symbolically enacted the return of Yahweh to Zion; Jesus took upon himself the role of messianic shepherd, Yahweh's role. According to Wright:

> As part of his human vocation, grasped in faith, sustained in prayer, tested in confrontation, agonized over in further prayer and doubt, and implemented in action, he believed he had to do and be, for Israel and the world, that which according to scripture only YHWH himself could do and be. He was Israel's Messiah; but there would, in the end, be "no king but God."

Jesus went to his death trusting against all odds that he was Israel's Messiah whom Yahweh would vindicate. There was no category for a crucified Messiah. Those messiahs who were crucified became by that very fact false messiahs. But Jesus trusted that this way, which he had to go alone, was Yahweh's way of saving Israel and thus the world. No wonder that he suffered agonies in the garden on the night he was betrayed. What a terrible risk he took! What if he were mistaken! But there in the Garden of Olives, all the evidence says, he was confirmed in his vocation and went into the lions' den trusting that Yahweh would vindicate him.

Was he vindicated? His disciples affirmed that he was raised from the dead. The only thing that makes historical sense of the rapid rise of Christianity is the resurrection. Within some twenty or thirty years of the crucifixion of Jesus, Paul could write: "If Christ has not been raised, your faith is futile and you are still in your sins. Then those also who have died in Christ have perished. If for this life only we have hoped in Christ, we are of all people most to be pitied" (1 Cor 15:17 –19). The earliest Christians lived with the conviction that they were in the messianic age, the last act of the story of Israel and thus of the world. They were distinguished by their love for one another and by their joy, even when they suffered horribly for their belief in Jesus. They believed that Jesus had been vindicated and that with his resurrection God had won his great victory.

Wright has a wonderful image. Israel's story has five acts, like a Shakespearean play. Creation is the first act; the fall is the second; the call of the Israelites is the third; Jesus' life, death and resurrection is the fourth; and now we are in the fifth. But the only way that we can bring the play to a conclusion is by acting it out. For the fifth act all we have for a script is the New Testament and, I would add, what Christians have done up to our part of the act. It is as if Shakespeare had written a play with four acts, leaving the fifth act to the players to finish from what they have learned through living through the first four. In other words, Jesus did not leave us with a set of beliefs so much as a task to carry out. We must live in faith what we believe, namely, that with Jesus' life, death and resurrection, the climactic work that God intends has been accomplished; we must live as an Easter people who follow the way of Jesus, the way of love, of peace, of the cross. We are to be the light of the world as followers of Jesus, the Jew of the first century who himself believed that he was God's final answer to our world's problems.

In the last three chapters we have been praying to know Jesus more intimately in order to love him more deeply and follow him more closely. We have encountered a remarkable, an extraordinary and a very challenging human being. Have we come to know him more intimately? If we have, then, I believe we cannot fail to love him more deeply. Each of us individually and all of us as the people of God, however, face the question of following him more closely. What does it mean for us as individuals and as a church to follow the way of Jesus in the changed circumstances of our time and given the history of how the story has been acted out in the centuries since the resurrection of Jesus? We are left with the task of discovering our vocation in our time and place just as Jesus discovered his vocation in his time and place. But we who know and love him have an advantage over him, namely, our knowledge and love of him.

Conclusion:
Shall We Dance?

Chapter 12

Intimacy with the Trinity

In the last three chapters we have come to know Jesus of Nazareth as a man with a unique vocation and with a unique consciousness of his relationship, indeed, of his oneness with God. To return to an image I used earlier, namely, that of the whirling dance of the Trinity, we might imagine this dancing presence of the triune God reaching a unique rhythmic and joyful exuberance in Jesus of Nazareth. In him alone of all human beings, we Christians profess, God was, and is, so intimately present that Jesus is, indeed, God, one of the three divine Persons. Jesus, the human being, the Jew of the first century, had such an intimate relationship with God that he was and is God. But he remained and remains a human being. We believe that he was raised from the dead, that his whole humanity is now with God. For a moment, let's reflect on the meaning of this belief.

A human being with physical, psychological, social and spiritual ties to the whole created universe is so one with God that he is God. This human being died and rose bodily from the dead. Everything in our created universe is interconnected. The more we learn about the universe, the more we recognize this fact of interconnectedness. The atomic and subatomic particles that are the stuff of the cosmos and everything in it are all interrelated and swirl through the whole universe. Our own human bodies constantly exchange particles and matter with the rest of the created universe. At the psychological and social levels of our beings we are interrelated; we stand on the shoulders of all those who have gone before us and have etched into our beings the marks of our forebears. At the spiritual level, too, we are all interconnected. We believe that the Jewish carpenter, Jesus of Nazareth, who is physically, psychologically, socially and spiritually interconnected with the whole universe, is risen from the dead. He is not someplace outside this universe. If he were, then he would not be bodily resurrected. The whole universe, therefore, is touched intimately with divinity. The dance of the Trinity in Jesus of Nazareth swirls through all of us and through the universe in some mysterious way. The music of God continues to play, promoting that dynamic movement that the Jesuit poet Gerard Manley Hopkins recognized when he wrote, "The world is charged with the grandeur of God." Already, therefore, before we become aware in faith of who we are, we are immersed in the music and dance of the Trinity; we are part of the great cosmic dance whose center is God.

Before his death Jesus promised that he would send his Spirit upon his disciples. In John's gospel that promise is fulfilled on the evening of his resurrection.

When it was evening on that day, the first day of the week, and the doors of the house where the disciples had met were locked for fear of the Jews, Jesus came and stood among them and said, "Peace be with you." After he said this, he showed them his hands and his side. Then the disciples rejoiced when they saw the Lord. Jesus said to them again, "Peace be with you. As the Father has sent me, so I send you." When he had said this, he breathed on them and said to them, "Receive the Holy Spirit. If you forgive the sins of any, they are forgiven them; if you retain the sins of any, they are retained." (Jn 20:19–23)

In the Acts of the Apostles the promise is fulfilled on the day of Pentecost.

When the day of Pentecost had come, they were all together in one place. And suddenly from heaven there came a sound like the rush of a violent wind, and it filled the entire house where they were sitting. Divided tongues, as of fire, appeared among them, and a tongue rested on each of them. All of them were filled with the Holy Spirit and began to speak in other languages, as the Spirit gave them ability. (Acts 2:1–4)

In the power of this Spirit of God the first disciples became the light of the world. They shared their goods with one another, spoke eloquently, witnessed fearlessly, lived joyously and suffered persecution gladly. In the power of this Spirit they cast out demons, healed the sick, raised the dead. In other words, in the power of the Spirit they were enabled to follow Jesus very closely and be his disciples, to live in this world in a way similar to his way of living. Christianity spread like wildfire throughout the Roman Empire and beyond. The dance of the Trinity became more and more evident and drew more and more people consciously into its rhythm. The church is the sacrament of that dance. With the resurrection of Jesus and the sending of the Holy Spirit a new day had, indeed, dawned. "This is the day that the Lord has made./ Let us rejoice and be glad."

We believe that the Spirit of God dwells in us, that we have been drawn into the divine life and movement. Once

again, let us reflect for a moment on this belief. At least
since the time of Pentecost, we believe, the Spirit of God
has dwelt in human beings like ourselves. We are drawn
into the intimate life of the Trinity by this indwelling Spirit.
Wherever we are, whether awake or asleep, whether conscious or not of the reality, the music and the dance of the
Trinity swirl around us. We are invited to become more
and more aware of the reality of being part of the inner
life of God, of God's choreography. This invitation is the
invitation to an intimate relationship with God, an invitation to become like Jesus in our relationship with God. Of
course, Jesus is unique; we are not so drawn into the dance
of the Trinity that we become divine. But we are invited
into as close an intimacy as possible. The more we become
conscious of being part of this dance, the happier we are.
We become more and more transparent to God and God
to us. We become more like Jesus. We also draw others to
want to join the dance with us or repel them, if they are
frightened by the nearness of God. We are the heirs of centuries of this cosmic, interpersonal dance. With all our
brothers and sisters throughout the world we are invited to
live consciously in this divine dance.

Our universe, our world, is not only the home of God
because Jesus of Nazareth is one with God and is risen, but
also because we, too, in our own way, are one with God
and will rise with Jesus. This universe, this world, in spite of
appearances, is where God dwells forever, where God rules
forever, where God loves with an everlasting love. Because
they became conscious that they were so intimately one
with the dance of God, the apostles were able to rejoice
"that they were considered worthy to suffer dishonor for
the sake of the name" (Acts 5:41), the Christian martyrs
were able to embrace their deaths with joy, saints like
Teresa of Avila were able to endure great pain with joy, the
Dutch Jewess Etty Hillesum was able to face her impending

death at the hands of the Nazis with peace, and countless ordinary men and women down the ages have been able to face pain and suffering with equanimity and courage. "If God is for us, who is against us?" (Rom 8:31).

Because this universe is where God dwells forever, where God dances forever, those who have died in Christ somehow live on with us. As the Letter to the Hebrews says: "Therefore, since we are surrounded by so great a cloud of witnesses, let us also lay aside every weight and the sin that clings so closely, and let us run with perseverance the race that is set before us, looking to Jesus the pioneer and perfecter of our faith, who for the sake of the joy that was set before him endured the cross, disregarding its shame, and has taken his seat at the right hand of the throne of God" (Heb 12:1–2). Our loved ones who have gone before us have not departed from this universe; they have joined more intimately in the dance of the Trinity, the same dance that carries the whole universe forward and of which we can become more conscious.

How do we become more conscious of the dance of the Trinity? I believe that we need to become more attuned to the spirits that move in our hearts. As we noted in the last chapter, Jesus believed that at every moment we are being pulled by opposing spirits, the Spirit of God and the evil spirit. Anne Morrow Lindbergh likened a mature relationship to a dance, two people moving to the same rhythm, creating a pattern together. "The joy of such a pattern is not only the joy of creation or the joy of participation, it is also the joy of living in the moment. Lightness of touch and living in the moment are intertwined." We are invited into such a mature relationship with God. We become more aware of the dance of the Trinity when we can live in the moment, not worrying about the past or the future. In *Spiritual Direction and the Encounter with God* I wrote:

...the experience of God as dance may reflect an encounter with God's one action which is the universe. That is, when our actions are in tune with God's one action with its intention that all human beings live as sisters and brothers, we experience ourselves in the flow, living in the present with a relative freedom from fear of the future or the past, and we address the mysterious Presence that we also encounter as Thou. When our actions are out of tune with God's one action, we experience a malaise, a disharmony, and if we let that disharmony into our consciousness, we know that we need help and we address "a higher Power," as the first step of Alcoholics Anonymous calls God, a Thou by whom alone we can be saved. But in addition, the experience of God as dance may reflect an encounter with God who is, quite apart from creation, the perfect dance, the mystery who is Three in One.

We discern the spirits in order to become more aware of the dance of God that is part and parcel of our universe.

Gerard Manley Hopkins, whom we met earlier in one of his darker days, was, it seems, saved from his darker moods because he believed and experienced the intimate presence of God in the world. So he could write the poem whose first line we cited earlier in this chapter.

The world is charged with the grandeur of God.
    It will flame out, like shining from shook foil;
    It gathers to a greatness, like the ooze of oil
Crushed. Why do men then now not reck his rod?
Generations have trod, have trod, have trod;
    And all is seared with trade; bleared, smeared
    with toil;

And wears man's smudge and shares man's smell:
the soil
Is bare now, nor can foot feel, being shod.

And, for all this, nature is never spent;
There lives the dearest freshness deep down
things;
And though the last lights off the black West went
Oh, morning, at the brown brink eastwards,
springs—
Because the Holy Ghost over the bent
World broods with warm breast and with ah!
bright wings.

We began this book asking what God wants and what
we want. God wants us to enter intimately and as consciously as possible the dance of his own inner life. God
has created a universe for this purpose, a purpose that is
for our peace. "I have loved you with an everlasting love."
Julian of Norwich ends her *Revelations* thus:

> From the time these things were first revealed I had
> often wanted to know what was our Lord's meaning.
> It was more than fifteen years after that I was
> answered in my spirit's understanding. "You would
> know our Lord's meaning in this thing? Know it well.
> Love was his meaning. Who showed it you? Love.
> What did he show you? Love. Why did he show it? For
> love. Hold on to this and you will know and under-
> stand love more and more. But you will not know or
> learn anything else—ever!"

So it was that I learned that love was our Lord's
meaning. And I saw for certain, both here and else-

where, that before ever he made us, God loved us;
and that his love has never slackened, nor ever shall.

At every moment we are invited into love's dance. God
invites us into such joy. And, as we find over and over
again, our deepest happiness and our only lasting peace is
to share the dance with God and with all whom we meet.
"Shall we dance?"

Bibliography

Anselm of Canterbury. Vol. 1, *Proslogion*. Eds. and trans. Jaspar Hopkins and Herbert Richardson. Toronto and New York: Edwin Mellen Press, 1974.

Augustine of Hippo. *Confession*. Trans. R. S. Pine-Coffin. Harmondsworth, England: Penguin, 1961.

Barnstone, Willis. *The Poems of Saint John of the Cross: English Versions and Introduction*. New York: New Directions, 1972.

Barry, William A. *Spiritual Direction and the Encounter with God: A Theological Inquiry*. New York/Mahwah, N. J.: Paulist Press, 1992.

———. *What Do I Want in Prayer?* New York/Mahwah, N. J.: Paulist Press, 1994.

———. *Who Do You Say I Am? Meeting the Historical Jesus in Prayer*. Notre Dame, Ind.: Ave Maria Press, 1996.

Becker, Ernest. *The Denial of Death*. New York: Free Press, 1973.

Brown, Peter R. L. *The Body and Society: Men, Women, and Sexual Renunciation in Early Christianity*. New York: Columbia University Press, 1988.

Buechner, Frederick. *The Longing for Home: Recollections and Reflections*. San Francisco: Harper & Row, 1996.

———. *The Sacred Journey*. San Francisco: Harper&Row, 1982.

Carmody, John Tully. *God Is No Illusion: Meditations on the End of Life*. Valley Forge, Pa.: Trinity Press International, 1997.

Clifford, Richard. *Deuteronomy with an Excursus on Covenant and Law: Old Testament Message,* vol. 4. Wilmington, Del.: Michael Glazier, 1989.

Cooley, Martha. *The Archivist.* Boston: Little, Brown, 1998.

Davies, Robertson. *The Cunning Man.* New York: Penguin, 1994.

Dubus, Andre. "Broken Vessels." In *Broken Vessels: Essays.* Boston: Godine, 1991.

———. "A Father's Story." In *The Times Are Never So Bad.* Boston: Godine, 1983.

Falk, Marcia. *The Song of Songs: A New Translation and Interpretation.* San Francisco: Harper & Row, 1990.

Green, Thomas H. *When the Well Runs Dry: Prayer Beyond the Beginnings.* New revised edition. Notre Dame, Ind.: Ave Maria Press, 1998.

Hanson, Ron. *Mariette in Ecstasy.* New York: HarperCollins, 1991.

Hassler, Jon, in James Martin, ed. *How Can I Find God? The Famous and the Not-So-Famous Consider the Quintessential Question.* Liguori, Mo.: Triumph Books, 1997.

Heaney, Seamus. *Death of a Naturalist.* London: Faber and Faber, 1966.

Hillesum, Etty. *An Interrupted Life: The Diaries of Etty Hillesum 1941–43.* New York: Washington Square Press, 1984.

Hopkins, Gerard Manley. *The Oxford Authors: Gerard Manley Hopkins.* Ed. Catherine Phillips. Oxford and New York: Oxford University Press, 1986.

Ignatius of Loyola. *The Spiritual Exercises of Saint Ignatius: A Translation and Commentary* by George E. Ganss, S.J. St. Louis: Institute of Jesuit Sources, 1992.

James, P. D. *Innocent Blood.* London: Penguin, 1989.

———. *Original Sin.* New York: Time Warner, 1994.

Julian of Norwich. *Revelations of Divine Love.* Trans. Clifton Wolters. Harmondsworth, England: Penguin, 1966.

Lewis, C. S. *The Pilgrim's Regress: An Allegorical Apology for*

Christianity, Reason and Romanticism. New York: Sheed & Ward, 1944.

———. *Surprised by Joy: The Shape of My Early Life.* London: Geoffrey Bles, 1955.

Lindbergh, Anne Morrow. *Gift from the Sea.* New York: Vintage Books, 1965.

May, Gerald G. *Care of Mind, Care of Spirit: Psychiatric Dimension of Spiritual Direction.* San Francisco: Harper & Row, 1982.

Meier, John. *A Marginal Jew: Rethinking the Historical Jesus. Vol. 1: The Roots of the Problem and the Person; vol. 2: Mentor, Message, and Miracles.* New York: Doubleday, 1991, 1994.

Moore, Sebastian. *Let This Mind Be in You: The Quest for Identity through Oedipus to Christ.* Minneapolis: Winston, 1985.

Nouwen, Henri M. *The Return of the Prodigal Son: A Story of Homecoming.* New York: Doubleday Image, 1994.

O'Connor, Flannery. *The Habit of Being: Letters.* Ed. Sally Fitzgerald. New York: Farrar, Straus, Giroux, 1979.

Otto, Rudolph. *The Idea of the Holy: An Inquiry into the Non-Rational Factor in the Idea of the Divine and Its Relation to the Rational.* Trans. John W. Harvey. London: Oxford University Press, 1976.

Pope, Marvin H. The Anchor Bible Series. *Song of Songs: A New Translation with Introduction and Commentary.* Garden City, N.Y.: Doubleday, 1977.

Speiser, E. A. The Anchor Bible Series. *Genesis: A New Translation with Introduction and Commentary.* Garden City, N.Y.: Doubleday, 1964.

Staudenmaier, John M. "To Fall in Love with the World: Individualism and Self-Transcendence in American Life." *Studies in the Spirituality of Jesuits* 26/3 (May, 1994).

Teresa of Avila. *The Collected Works of St. Teresa of Avila.* *Vols. 1, 2.* Trans. Kieran Kavanaugh and Otilio Rodriguez. Washington, D.C.: Institute of Carmelite Studies, 1976.

Terrien, Samuel. *The Elusive Presence: Toward a Biblical Theology.* San Francisco: Harper & Row, 1978.

Tolkien, J. R. R. *The Fellowship of the Ring.* New York: Ballantine, 1973.

Vacek, Edward. "Religious Life and the Eclipse of the Love for God." *Review for Religious* 57/2 (March-April, 1998): 118–137.

Wright, N. T. *Christian Origins and the Question of God. Vol. 1: The New Testament and the People of God; vol. 2: Jesus and the Victory of God.* Minneapolis: Fortress Press, 1992, 1996.

———. "How Jesus Saw Himself." *Bible Review* 12/3 (1966), 22–29.